Wild Flowers

HAMLYN JUNIOR POCKET BOOKS

Wild
Flowers

ANN BONAR
ILLUSTRATED BY CYNTHIA POW

HAMLYN
LONDON · NEW YORK · SYDNEY · TORONTO

Acknowledgements

Photographs
Bruce Coleman, Uxbridge: Hans Reinhard front cover; Natural
History Photographic Agency, Hythe: J. & M. Bain & G.J.
Cambridge 51, 62, 66, 114, Arthur Butler 14, 19, 23, 47, 87, N.R.
Coulton 58, Stephen Dalton 2–3, 15, 26, 27, 35, 38, 59, 71, 78, 83,
90, 91, 95, 106, 107, 119, 122, Brian Hawkes 42, 115, G.E. Hyde
94, E.A. Janes 30, 63, 111, 118, J. Jeffrey 75, Tom Jenkyn 102,
R.W.S. Knightbridge 82, David M. Manners 31, K.G. Preston-
Mafham 22, 50, 55, 110; Joan Small, London 18, 34, 39, 43, 46,
54, 70, 79, 86, 98, 99, 103; Mary Stevens, Kingston-upon-Thames
74.

The front cover picture shows Ox-eye Daisy (*Leucanthemum
vulgare*), Harebell (*Campanula rotundifolia*), Ragged Robin
(*Lychnis flos-cuculae*), Field Scabious (*Knautia arvensis*) and Bistort
(*Polygonum bistorta*).

The title page picture shows Field Scabious (*Knautia arvensis*).

First published 1982 by
The Hamlyn Publishing Group Limited
London · New York · Sydney · Toronto
Astronaut House, Feltham, Middlesex, England

ISBN 0 600 36451 8
Printed in Italy

Contents

Introduction

When you go for a walk – in the country, through a park or across a common or heath – you will always see plants growing which have not been specially planted. Mostly they are called wild plants, but if you see them growing in a garden, they will be called weeds.

Dandelions, Daisies, Nettles – these are some of the commonest weeds, but they are in fact plants native to northern Europe; they were not brought here originally by plant collectors, as many kinds of garden plants and trees were, but have grown here naturally for millions of years.

Some plants which were introduced for garden cultivation several hundred years ago have adapted to growing in northern Europe so much that they have seeded and spread from gardens into the wild. This is known as naturalizing, and they now grow as much and as well as the native plants.

Naming plants

Because there are so many plants, and because people from so many countries want to study them and learn about them, they have been given botanic names, in Latin, which are used throughout the world. You can call them by their common names if you like, but if you want to be really specific about which wild plant you are discussing, it is better to use the botanic name, because the common name changes from area to area, and from country to country. While Ground Elder has lots of common names, such as Jack-jump-about, Pigweed and Bishop's Weed, its botanic name of *Aegopodium podagraria* is recognized everywhere.

The botanic name is in two parts. Plants have a surname and a Christian name, like you do, but the surname comes first. This shows which group, or *genus* as it is called, the plant belongs to. The Dandelion's botanic surname is *Taraxacum* (its *generic* name), but because there are several similar plants in this genus, the Dandelion is called *Taraxacum officinale*, to separate it from the others. Its Christian name is known as its *species* or *specific* name. So a plant's full name can look like this:

Dandelion   (*Taraxacum officinale*)
(Common name)   (Genus)   (Species)

Just one other thing to remember: each genus (plural, genera) is also part of a bigger group, where the plants all have some parts which are alike. This is called a family, the name of which always ends in 'ae' as you will see when you look through the book. The Dandelion belongs to the family *Compositae* which also includes plants such as the Daisies and Thistles.

You might be wondering why plants have been put into the groups they are in – why a particular collection are in one family, and another set are in another family. The main reason is all to do with the flowers. The dividing up, or classifying of flowering plants, as it is called, depends on what the flowers are like, and also the fruits and seeds.

PARTS OF A TYPICAL FLOWERING PLANT

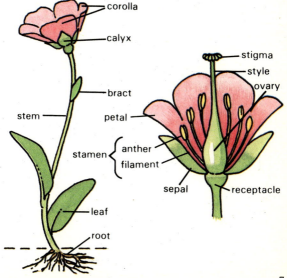

How to use this book

When you find a wild plant that you do not know the name of, in order to name it, you need to look closely at the flower to see how many petals it has, the number of stamens, what its calyx is like, and the kind of flower cluster. You also need to note things like the plant's height, the time of flowering, what its fruit or seed pods look like, and anything else you can see: hairs, prickles; its habit of growth (whether it is bushy, tall, climbing, or creeps along the ground); and so on, even whether it is scented (sweet-smelling) or aromatic (spicy-smelling). Don't forget to examine the leaves; their appearance helps, even if it is not essential in identification.

You will find in the descriptions of the plants in this book that the most important details of their appearance are given, the ones which will be of most help in deciding what plant it is that you have just found. The different botanical terms used in describing plants are explained in the glossary (see pp. 12–13).

When you have found a plant and don't know its name, turn to the section of the book with flowers of the same colour. Sometimes flowers can vary a lot in colour from one plant to another, so when you have a purple flower, it may be in the lilac section in this book, and so on with other colours. Then decide on the flower structure and look under that type of appearance within the colour section. The different flower types are as follows: *grouped flowers* – these are small flowers which are not easy to examine individually and which may be in stalked clusters like Cow Parsley, or in leafy whorls like Mint, or in globular heads like Clover, or in composite heads of florets like Dandelions, Daisies and Thistles, or in spikes like Sorrel and Twayblade; open flowers with clearly visible petals – these are divided up by petal number into *six or more petals*, *five petals*, *four petals*, *three petals*; *two-lipped/peaflowers* such as Honeysuckle and Vetch; and *bell-shaped* flowers. Any flowers which do not fit into these types will appear at the end of each colour section.

Once you think you have found the name of the flower, check that the flowering period is the same; that the leaf shape is the same; and finally that the plant is growing in the right kind of place (the habitat). There are five different habitats:

FLOWER TYPES

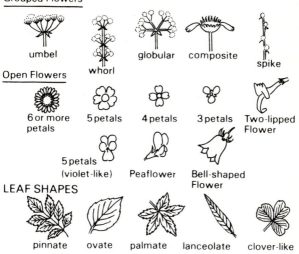

Grouped Flowers

umbel

whorl

globular

composite

spike

Open Flowers

6 or more petals

5 petals

4 petals

3 petals

Two-lipped Flower

5 petals (violet-like)

Peaflower

Bell-shaped Flower

LEAF SHAPES

pinnate

ovate

palmate

lanceolate

clover-like

fields/wasteland/hedgerows; shady places/woodland; damp places/water; high places/mountains; coast/seashore. Sometimes plants will grow in more than one kind of place, so if you don't find the plant in one habitat, go on looking in others.

High places includes moors; coasts includes sea-cliffs; and damp places means beside streams, ponds or lakes, or in bogs or marshes. Wasteland includes paths, roadsides, waste-heaps, quarries, any kind of ground not used for growing crops.

You can eat parts of some plants, but other plants are very poisonous and should not be eaten. Therefore, you should always check with an adult before you eat any part of any plant.

KEY	*Throughout the captions to illustrations, the following abbreviations have been used.*		
F = flowers	Fs = flower spikes	(f) = female	
C = clusters	mm = millimetres	x = across	
Fh = flowerheads	(m) = male	l = long	

Keeping records

After you have discovered what a plant is called, you might like to start writing down its name and those of other plants in an exercise book, together with a description of what they look like, where you found them and the date. So for each plant you could have:

Name	Description of flowers
Habitat	Description of leaves
Place found	Description of seed pods
Date	or fruit
Habit of growth	Height

If you are good at drawing, you could do a sketch next to the written description, otherwise perhaps someone would take a photograph, which you could stick into your book.

If there are lots of specimens of the plant growing where you found it, you can pick one and press it, **but only if there are lots**. You must never dig up a whole plant; it is against the law to do so unless you have the landowner's permission. For pressing, you need only a flower, part of the stem with two or three leaves on it, and the seedpods or fruit. Lay them flat between two sheets of absorbent paper, put a heavy weight on top, and after a few weeks the parts will have dried.

Then you can transfer it carefully to a clean sheet of paper, at least 28 centimetres long and 22 centimetres wide, and stick it down with small pieces of gummed paperstrip. If you collect specimens like this, you will need a hard-covered loose-leaf file.

How plants live

Once you begin to look at plants, and perhaps collect and record them, you will begin to understand that they are not just bits of the scenery, as stones or streams are, but are things with life in them. Plants grow bigger, and they need air, food and water in the same way that you do. Their big difference from animals is that they cannot move about.

A plant feeds in two ways. One is to take in food through its roots from the soil. This food consists of tiny particles of such substances as copper, sulphur, iron, phosphorus and many others, which are dissolved in the water in the soil. This water is sucked in by the roots, and the food particles are then used in the plant's 'body': its stems, leaves and flowers. This method of feeding is also the plant's method of drinking and is the way in which it gets the water it needs.

Plants also make food, within their leaves, from the air by combining the carbon-dioxide in it with water to produce starch and oxygen. When this process does not produce as much oxygen as plants need to 'breathe', they do so by absorbing oxygen from the air through all their surfaces.

Using plants

Plants are extremely useful to man, and humans would not be able to live without them. For example, grasses and clovers are two of the main foods of cows and sheep, which supply us with beef, mutton, cheese, milk and butter, as well as wool and leather. Chickens feed on the grain from Wheat and Maize, seeds of other plants, grasses and various 'weeds'; they in turn provide meat and eggs.

Bread is made from all sorts of *cereals*: Wheat, Barley, Rye and Oat seeds. *Vegetables* are the leaves, roots and seed heads, and sometimes the flowers, of various plants, and *fruits*, such as strawberries and apples, are the seed containers of other plants.

But parts of plants are also used for curing illness and healing injuries; these are often called *herbs*. Many other plants provide fibres and material for clothing, for example Flax provides linen, cotton comes from the seed head of a plant, and hemp and jute are obtained by special treatment of various tropical plants. The perfumes of Lavender, Violet and Rose are a few of the many extracted from flowers, and blue, yellow and brown dyes come from Woad, Dyer's Greenweed and Walnut respectively.

So you see, plants are very important, and you should always treat and handle them carefully, so that they can go on living and growing.

Glossary

Alternate Describes leaves which are produced singly on a stem, from one side or the other in turn.

Annual A plant which germinates, flowers and sets seed, all within one growing season.

Anther The part of a flower which produces pollen.

Biennial A plant which produces roots and leaves in one year, then flowers in the second year, and dies after flowering.

Bract Usually looks like a green leaf, at the base of a flower, its stalk, or the stalk of a cluster of flowers; sometimes it is large and coloured, looking like a petal.

Bulb A kind of underground bud, whose undeveloped leaves are swollen with food to be stored while the plant rests.

Calyx The outer 'petals' of a flower, which are in fact the sepals, and are often green and much smaller than the true petals.

Carnivorous Such a plant feeds on insects, usually by means of its leaves.

Chlorophyll The green colouring matter of plants. It can only be formed in daylight.

Corm Like a bulb, but the swollen or thickened part is a stem, not leaves, and there are no overlapping layers.

Family The name for a group of plants which has various characteristics which are the same in each plant.

Filament The thin 'stems' inside the flower; at the top of them are the pollen containers (anthers).

Genus A collection of plants which have developed from the same origin and therefore are very similar.

Lanceolate Describes leaves which are long and narrow, with one or both ends long and pointed.

Leaflet Many leaves consist of several smaller parts or leaflets, which should never be called leaves.

Oblong Describes leaves which are long and almost rectangular, but more rounded.

Opposite Describes leaves which are produced two at a time at the same point on the stem, but on opposite sides of it.

Ovate Describes egg-shaped leaves with the widest part of each leaf nearest its stalk.

Palmate Describes a leaf divided into several parts so that it looks like a hand held out flat.

Parasite A plant which feeds on other plants which are still living.

Perennial A plant which lives for three years or longer.

Petal Usually the coloured 'showy' part of a flower, though sometimes petals are small and green, or their colour and size make them insignificant.

Pinnate Describes feathery leaves which consist of two rows of leaflets, one on each side of a central stalk, regularly arranged and more or less all the same size.

Pollen The powder-like grains, looking like dust, found in small sacs at the ends of the anthers.

Rhizome A creeping stem which grows under the soil.

Rosette A cluster of leaves without stalks, coming straight out of the soil, or straight out of a branch or stem.

Saprophyte A plant which feeds on other plants which are dead or dying.

Sepal The parts which make up the calyx and are often green; they enclose the flower bud. They can also look just like the petals, but are on the outside of the flower.

Species A member of a genus. The seeds of one species will produce plants exactly like the parent plant.

Spike A long flowerhead whose flowers are very close together and have either very short stalks or none.

Stamen The part of a flower which carries the pollen; it consists of the filament and the anther.

Stigma The sticky part at the top of the style.

Style The style is the thin central stem within the flower, leading down to the part where the seeds will develop. There may be more than one per flower.

Toothed Describes the edge or margin of leaves which have jagged points on them.

Tuber A swollen rounded root, sometimes a stem, often in the soil.

Whorl Leaves or flowers arranged like this are in a circular cluster of three or more, from a single place on the stem.

Wort Derived from an Anglo-Saxon word, *wyrt*, meaning a herb in the sense of a non-woody plant; often used of vegetables as well as in wild flower common names.

Yellow Flowers

Black Medick
F 2-5mm l
▽

Cudweed
C 12mm x
◁

Crosswort
F 2-2.5mm x
◁

Coltsfoot
Fh 15-35mm x
▽

△
Fleabane
Fh 15-30mm x

Groundsel
Fh 6-10mm x
▷

Dandelion
Fh 35-50mm x
◁

Hawk's-beard
Fh 15-25mm x
▷

GROUPED FLOWERS

Black Medick
(Medicago lupulina)

Fields/wasteland/hedgerows
Leguminosae

A plant with low creeping stems, leaves with three leaflets, and tiny yellow flowers, 10–50 appearing in a round head late in spring, or in summer. The seeds are black when ripe. Often found in lawns, like Bird's-Foot Trefoil. **Annual**

Coltsfoot
(Tussilago farfara)

Fields/wasteland/hedgerows
Compositae

Prefers chalky soil. Coltsfoot has large, 12 centimetres wide, heart-shaped leaves (like an animal's hoof-print), slightly toothed and with a white underside. Single, yellow daisy-like flowers, on 15 centimetres long stems, bloom in March before the leaves appear. **Perennial**

Crosswort
(Cruciata laevipes)

Fields/wasteland/hedgerows
Rubiaceae

The delicate flowering stems of this hairy plant appear between April and early June, and grow to about 30 centimetres tall. The small pointed leaves grow in clusters of four up the stem, and the tiny, star-like scented flowers also grow in clusters with the leaves. **Perennial**

Cudweed
(Filago vulgaris)

Fields/wasteland/hedgerows
Compositae

You will have to look carefully for this, as it is a small low-growing plant, easily missed. The whole plant is whitish green, as it is covered in a white down. The 6 millimetres long leaves are narrow, and the flowers come in clusters, appearing to be yellow but actually white with red tips, from July to August. **Annual**

Dandelion

(Taraxacum officinale)

Fields/wasteland/hedges
Compositae

The Dandelion's round, bright yellow flowers can be seen everywhere during spring and summer, on stems 2.5–15 centimetres tall. Its long leaves form a rosette and have toothed lobes. Its name comes from the French words *dents de lion*, meaning lion's teeth. The seedhead forms a powder-puff-like dandelion 'clock', each seed of which has a fluffy end for wind dispersal.

Perennial

Fleabane

(Pulicaria dysenterica)

Damp places/water
Compositae

The clusters of 2–3 centimetres wide, yellow 'daisies' which are characteristic of Fleabane appear from July to September at the top of stems 30–60 centimetres long. The plant is softly woolly all over and greyish green, with oblong wavy-edged leaves. If the plant is burnt, the smoke is said to drive away fleas.

Annual

Groundsel

(Senecio vulgaris)

Fields/wasteland/hedgerows
Compositae

This is a very common plant; you will probably find it in the garden, especially in the vegetable garden, where it is thought of as a weed. It is a small plant, up to about 15 centimetres tall, with pinnate leaves – the lobes of which are toothed – and clusters of small, yellow, brush-like flowers almost all year.

Annual

Hawk's-beard

(Crepis vesicaria)

Fields/wasteland/hedgerows
Compositae

You will see Hawk's-beard flowering by the sides of fields and footpaths from May to July. Clusters of dandelion-like yellow flowers, each 1.5–2.5 centimetres wide, appear at the top of stems 45 centimetres long; the leaves also look like those of Dandelions. Identify it by the outside ring of green bracts, which have whitish edges, and are quite short. **Biennial**

△
Lesser Hawkbit
Fh 12-20mm x

Lady's Bedstraw
C 5-20mm x
▷

Hawkweed
Fh 15-30mm x
◁

△
Hop Trefoil
F 4-5mm l

Sowthistle
Fh 15-25mm x
▽

Nipplewort
Fh up to 20mm x
▽

Ragwort
Fh 25mm x

Tansy
Fh 7-10mm x
▽

Hawkweed
(*Hieracium* species)

Fields/wasteland/hedgerows
Compositae

There are lots of Hawkweeds, looking very alike, but generally they have flowers in clusters during the summer like the Hawk's-beards; the leaves are different, long and narrow, slightly toothed and not lobed. The fluffy seedheads are pale brown. *Hieracium* comes from the Greek word *hierax*, a hawk.

Perennial

Hop Trefoil
(*Trifolium campestre*)

Fields/wasteland/hedgerows
Leguminosae

A trefoil with rounded heads of small yellow flowers, 20–30 in a cluster on creeping or upright stems 15–30 centimetres long and leaves with three leaflets. The flowers turn brown when they die, but do not drop. Flowering is mainly in summer (from May to September). Hop Trefoil grows mostly in dry places and, like the other trefoils and Black Medick, is a lawn weed.

Annual

Lady's Bedstraw
(*Galium verum*)

Fields/wasteland/hedgerows
Rubiaceae

In dry summers, this plant thrives; it does not need much water. It has delicate stems, rather sprawling, about 20 centimetres long, and narrow pointed leaves in groups of 8–12. The tiny, star-like yellow flowers are in spiky clusters. In ancient times it was used to colour cheese yellow and flavour it, and also to curdle milk.

Perennial

Lesser Hawkbit
(*Leontodon taraxacoides*)

Fields/wasteland/hedgerows
Compositae

The flowers look like those of Hawk's-beard, but there is only one on each stem, and the long, narrow leaves, coarsely toothed, grow in a rosette at the base of the plant. The stems are 15–30 centimetres long, and flowers appear summer and autumn. It is called Hawkbit because it was once believed that hawks ate the plant to improve their sight.

Perennial

Nipplewort
(Lapsana communis)

Fields/wasteland/hedgerows
Compositae

Common everywhere, you will see the small, yellow, rather daisy-like flowers any time between June and October. The stalked clusters of only a few flowers are at the top of stems 20–90 centimetres tall; hairy leaves are long-pointed, sometimes toothed. They taste like radishes and can be eaten in salads. **Annual**

Ragwort
(Senecio jacobaea)

Fields/wasteland/hedgerows
Compositae

Ragwort grows to about 60–90 centimetres tall, and has golden-yellow daisy-type flowers in clusters at the top of the stems, from July into October. In summer you may find black and yellow striped caterpillars eating the leaves, which are rather feathery and toothed. Ragwort is poisonous to farm animals. **Biennial**

Sowthistle
(Sonchus oleraceus)

Fields/wasteland/hedgerows
Compositae

Like Dandelion, Sowthistle has a 'clock' for a seedhead. The stems are 30–90 centimetres long and thick, but hollow, containing a milky juice when broken. The leaves are oblong, with prickly teeth on the edges, and pale yellow flowers, 1.2–2.5 centimetres wide, in clusters. Sowthistle leaves and stems are the favourite food of rabbits, and pigs also like them. Flowering time is from May to November. **Annual**

Tansy
(Tanacetum vulgare)

Fields/wasteland/hedgerows
Compositae

Tansy pancakes were very popular during the Middle Ages, for eating at Easter, made with the bright yellow, button-like flowers. The Tansy plant is tall, 90 centimetres, with tough stems, and very feathery, dark green leaves. The clusters of flowers appear from August to September. The whole plant has a strong, aromatic smell. **Perennial**

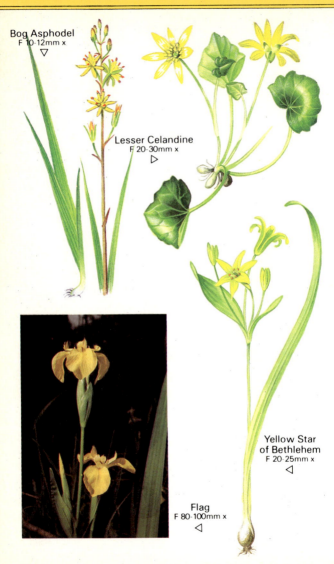

Bog Asphodel
F 10-12mm x
▽

Lesser Celandine
F 20-30mm x
▷

**Yellow Star
of Bethlehem**
F 20-25mm x
◁

Flag
F 80-100mm x
◁

22

Yellow-wort
F 18-22mm x
▷

Cowslip
F 10-15mm x
▽

Common Mullein
F 12-35mm x

Agrimony
F 5-8mm x
▷

SIX OR MORE PETALS

Bog Asphodel
(Narthecium ossifragum)

Damp places/water
Liliaceae

Look for this in bogs, particularly in the north and west. The yellow star-like flowers have orange anthers and are six-petalled, in spikes at the end of 15–30 centimetre long stems. It flowers from July to September. The leaves look like iris leaves, and the fruit are deep orange. **Perennial**

Flag (Yellow Iris)
(Iris pseudocorus)

Damp places/water
Iridaceae

You will find this growing mostly at the edge of streams, canals and ponds, and the six-petalled flowers bloom any time in June and July. Height is about 90 centimetres, the leaves are long, narrow and pointed, and each seed pod (there are three to a flower) is oblong, up to 7 centimetres long, with brown seeds inside it. **Perennial**

Lesser Celandine
(Ranunculus ficaria)

Damp places/water
Ranunculaceae

A small pretty plant whose yellow 8–12 petalled flowers grow straight out of the ground on stems 7–12 centimetres high. Leaves are heart-shaped and shiny, and it has small tubers. It appears in spring, but dies down in May completely until the next spring. *Ranunculus* is the Latin word for 'little frog'; many of this family grow in wet places. **Perennial**

Yellow Star of Bethlehem
(Gagea lutea)

Fields/wasteland/hedgerows
Liliaceae

Look for this uncommon plant in sandy soil or open woods. The bluebell-like leaves come from a tiny bulb like a large pea, and the flowering stem grows to about 12 centimetres tall. The flowers are six-petalled with a green stripe on the outside, only opening at midday. Flowers from March to April.

Perennial

Yellow-wort
(Blackstonia perfoliata)

Fields/wasteland/hedgerows
Gentianaceae

Perfoliata means 'through the leaves', and the stem does appear to pierce through pairs of the long, triangular leaves, the veins of which are parallel (most plants have the veins of the leaves in a network). Height 7–30 centimetres, and flowers three to four in a cluster, yellow, with about eight petal-like lobes from a short tube, appearing from June to October, sometimes on sand dunes.   **Annual**

FIVE PETALS

Agrimony
(Agrimonia eupatoria)

Fields/wasteland/hedgerows
Rosaceae

Agrimony is a very common wayside plant which has tiny bright yellow five-petalled flowers appearing in a long spike, from June to autumn. Height 60–90 centimetres; most of the pinnate leaves grow in a basal rosette, and have two to five pairs of toothed leaflets. Stems and leaves are softly hairy. It was once used for healing wounds.   **Perennial**

Common Mullein
(Verbascum thapsus)

Fields/wasteland/hedgerows
Scrophulariaceae

Tall plants, up to about 120 centimetres, covered in white 'wool'. Leaves oblong, lower ones large and 15–20 centimetres long. Bright yellow flowers in long dense spikes appearing from June to August.   **Biennial**

Cowslip
(Primula veris)

Fields/wasteland/hedgerows
Primulaceae

The Cowslip has a cluster of small, deep yellow flowers, like small Primroses, at the top of a stem 10–15 centimetres long, and flowers in April; sometimes you will find one with brick-red flowers. Look for them growing amongst short grass in hilly places. Cowslips were once the most important flower used to decorate the Maypole on Mayday.   **Perennial**

Creeping Buttercup
F 20mm x
▽

Kingcup
F 10-50mm x
▽

Creeping Cinquefoil
F 17-25mm x
▽

Field Buttercup
F 18-27mm x
▽

Primrose
F 20-30mm x
▷

Rock-rose
F 20-25mm x
▽

Tutsan
F about 20mm x
▷

Silverweed
F 15-20mm x
▷

Wall Pepper
F 12mm x
◁

27

Creeping Buttercup
(Ranunculus repens)

Fields/wasteland/hedgerows
Ranunculaceae

This buttercup often grows in damp meadows, and produces long, creeping stems with a plantlet on the end, which roots and then repeats the process. Its leaves are more clearly lobed than the Field Buttercup, and the middle one is stalked. Height 30–60 centimetres, flowering from May to August.

Perennial

Creeping Cinquefoil
(Potentilla reptans)

Fields/wasteland/hedgerows
Rosaceae

This plant has low-growing stems, which root at the leaf-joints, and palmate leaves with five to seven toothed leaflets. The yellow five-petalled flowers come singly, not clustered, on long stalks of about 10 centimetres, flowering from June to September. Creeping Cinquefoil likes chalky soil.   **Perennial**

Field Buttercup (Crowfoot)
(Ranunculus acris)

Fields/wasteland/hedgerows
Ranunculaceae

The Field Buttercup is one of the commonest meadow plants, with toothed, two-to-seven-lobed lower leaves, and fern-like upper leaves. Yellow, five-petalled flowers appear at the tops of stems 30–90 centimetres long in spring and summer. It was once thought to help the flow of milk from cows and improve the butter content.   **Perennial**

Kingcup (Marsh Marigold)
(Caltha palustris)

Damp places/water
Ranunculaceae

If you see a flower looking like a gigantic Buttercup, growing close to or in streams, it is probably the Kingcup. Deep yellow, with fleshy stems 30–60 centimetres long, and shiny, kidney-shaped, dark green leaves, it has five-petalled flowers from mid-March to mid-June. It was once thought to be a charm against the lightning of May storms.   **Perennial**

Primrose
(Primula vulgaris)

Shady places/woodland
Primulaceae

The name comes from the Latin, *primus ver*, meaning the 'first of the spring'. It flowers from February to May. The fragrant flowers are yellow, usually one on each delicate pinkish stem about 8 centimetres long. **Perennial**

Rock-rose
(Helianthemum nummularium)

Fields/wasteland/hedgerows
Cistaceae

The Rock-rose is a creeping plant with tough stems and small, narrow dark green leaves in pairs. The flower stems are about 9–30 centimetres tall, with bright yellow, five-petalled blooms appearing from May to September. **Perennial**

Silverweed
(Potentilla anserina)

Fields/wasteland/hedgerows
Rosaceae

The silver-green feathery toothed leaves grow 5–12 centimetres long, on runner-like stems which root at the leaf-joints. Yellow, five-petalled flowers up to 2 centimetres wide come singly, not in clusters, between May and August. **Perennial**

Tutsan
(Hypericum androsaemum)

Shady places/woodland
Guttiferae

In autumn this short (45 centimetres), shrubby evergreen has lots of red, green and black berries all mixed up together. The five-petalled flowers are about 2 centimetres wide, with many stamens, and appear from June to August; the leaves are ovate, without stems, and in pairs. **Perennial**

Wall Pepper (Biting Stonecrop)
(Sedum acre)

Fields/wasteland/hedgerows
Crassulaceae

Wall Pepper forms mats of creeping stems a few centimetres long, over rocks, with peppery tasting, tiny, fleshy rounded leaves all along them. Star-shaped five-petalled flowers, 1.2 centimetres wide, bloom during July and August. **Perennial**

Yellow Loosestrife
F 15-20mm x
△

Black Mustard
F 15mm x
△

Wood Avens
F 8-15mm x
◁

Yellow Waterlily
F 50-70mm x
△

White Mustard
F 20mm x
◁

Greater Celandine
F 25mm x
▽

Yellow Horned Poppy
F 60-90mm x
▽

Yellow Bird's Nest △
F 15mm x

Wood Avens
(Geum urbanum)

Shady places/woodland
Rosaceae

Once called St Benedict's Herb, this grows 30–60 centimetres tall, has short, alternate, pinnate dark green leaves, and upright yellow flowers with five petals, appearing from May to September. Each crimson seed has a long curved hook.

Perennial

Yellow Loosestrife
(Lysimachia vulgaris)

Damp places/water
Primulaceae

Loosestrife got its common name because it was once used to keep cows and oxen placid – it drives away biting insects. This 'Yellow Pimpernel' grows 60–90 centimetres tall, has two to four long, pointed leaves in clusters, and stalked yellow flowers in leafy groups, each with five pointed lobes looking like petals. Flowering time is from July to August. **Perennial**

Yellow Waterlily
(Spatterdock) *(Nuphar lutea)*

Fields/wasteland/hedgerows
Cruciferae

Whereas the white Waterlily has pointed petals, this has much fewer, rounded ones, usually five, or six, forming a flower 7 centimetres across. Flowering time is from June to September. The leaves are oval, 40 centimetres wide and floating; the plant grows in quite deep, still or slow-flowing water. **Perennial**

FOUR PETALS

Black Mustard
(Brassica nigra)

Fields/wasteland/hedgerows
Cruciferae

The seeds have a very hot, burning flavour and were used to make the original Old English mustard. The plant is tall, 90–180 centimetres, hairy and greyish green, with lobed, deeply divided basal leaves, and small (1.5 centimetres across) yellow flowers appearing in stalked clusters from July to September. The seed pods are 1.2 centimetres long closely pressed against the stems. The seeds are black. **Annual**

Greater Celandine
(Chelidonium majus)

Fields/wasteland/hedgerows
Papaveraceae

Once called Swallow-wort, and a member of the Poppy family, this plant flowers from spring into autumn. Look for its four-petalled 2.5 centimetres wide flowers on stems 30–60 centimetres tall growing from walls as well as beneath hedges. The grey-green leaves are pinnate with rounded teeth. If the stem is broken, it will ooze orange coloured juice. **Perennial**

White Mustard
(Sinapis alba)

Fields/wasteland/hedgerows
Cruciferae

Much shorter growing than Black Mustard, up to only 30 centimetres or so. All leaves are deeply lobed and divided, the flowers are 2 centimetres wide, and the seed pods markedly bumpy. The seeds are creamy beige in colour. Time of flowering is from April to October. This is the seed used as part of the mustard-and-cress mixture. **Annual**

Yellow Bird's Nest
(Monotropa hypopitys)

Shady places/woodland
Monotropaceae

A saprophytic plant which lives on rotting leaves and twigs. You are most likely to find it in beech or pine woods. Stems are 10–20 centimetres long, with scale-like leaves close against them, all a creamy colour but later turning pale brown. Tubular, pale yellow flowers appear on arching short spikes from June to August. **Perennial**

Yellow Horned Poppy
(Glaucium flavum)

Coast/seashore
Papaveraceae

Large, yellow, poppy-like flowers on short stems are typical of this species; they have four petals and are 6–9 centimetres wide, blooming from June to September. The hairy grey-green leaves are fern-like, and the seed pods very long, up to 30 centimetres. This poppy grows directly out of shingle or sand on the beach, as well as inland. If the stems or leaves are broken, sticky yellow juice oozes out. **Perennial/biennial**

Gorse
F 10-15mm l
▽

Bladderwort
F 20-30mm l
▷

Broom
F 20-25mm l
▽

Bird's-foot Trefoil
F 8-15mm l
▽

△
Honeysuckle
F 30-40mm l

△
Melilot
F 4-6mm l

Monkey Flower
F 25-45mm l
▷

TWO-LIPPED/PEAFLOWERS

Bird's-foot Trefoil
(Lotus corniculatus)

Fields/wasteland/hedgerows
Leguminosae

The seed pods of this plant are straight, 2.5 centimetres long, in a cluster looking like a bird's foot. Leaflets are in fives, but the two lower ones are not very obvious. The stems lie along the ground, with two to seven yellow flowers in a head, often tinted orange or red. Look for them from May to September.

Perennial

Bladderwort
(Utricularia vulgaris)

Damp places/water
Lentibulariaceae

Bladderwort floats on the water surface, it has no roots, and the leaves are thread-like, with small, air-filled bladders on them. The flowers are yellow, rather large, at the top of stems 15–20 centimetres long, appearing in July and August. It is carnivorous; each bladder has a trap which opens when its prey, such as water-fleas, swims close to it, and is sucked in, to be digested and absorbed.

Perennial

Broom
(Cytisus scoparius)

Fields/wasteland/hedgerows
Leguminosae

In olden times the twigs, being stiff and wiry, were bundled together and really were used as brooms. This is a shrub, up to 1.8 metres tall, with very few leaves, each having three leaflets; the yellow flowers appear in spikes from April to June. Dry or rocky heath-like places are its habitat. It used to be a symbol of good luck.

Perennial

Gorse (Furze)
(Ulex europaeus)

Fields/wasteland/hedgerows
Leguminosae

An extremely prickly shrub, any height from 30–150 centimetres tall, with dark green stems. Gorse has no leaves – these have been reduced to spines, amongst which you will find the yellow peaflowers at the top of the stems. They have an almond scent, and can be found almost all year round.

Perennial

Honeysuckle (Woodbine)

(Lonicera periclymenum)

Shady places/woodland
Caprifoliaceae

Honeysuckle is quickly tracked down in July and August by the strong perfume from its creamy yellow flowers, and it is often still flowering in October. It is found in hedges, twined amongst Hawthorn or Blackthorn. The plant produces red berries which are poisonous. Woodbine is one of its common names because it twines, or binds, itself round trees.

Perennial

Melilot

(Melilotus officinalis)

Fields/wasteland/hedgerows
Leguminosae

This was a common crop for feeding horses and cows during Elizabethan times, and bees are attracted to it because it has very sweet nectar. The plant grows to a height of 60–120 centimetres, and has leaves with three leaflets like the trefoils, and several long spikes of stalked flowers from July to September. When dried, it has a strongly aromatic fragrance.

Biennial

Monkey Flower

(Mimulus guttatus)

Damp places/water
Scrophulariaceae

This is grown in gardens, but it now grows wild as well, and you will often find it flowering all summer by streams and rivers throughout Britain. Not very tall, the fleshy creeping stems may turn upwards 20 or 25 centimetres. The shiny, ovate, pointed leaves are toothed, in pairs, and the yellow trumpet-like flowers have red spots in the throat and often on the lower lip.

Perennial

Spotted Medick
F 5-7mm l

Yellow Bartsia
F 15-30mm l

Yellow Archangel
F about 15mm x

Toadflax
F 15-30mm l

Comfrey
F about 16mm x
▽

△
Creeping Jenny
F 15-25mm x

Yellow Corydalis
F about 15mm l
◁

Daffodil
F 50mm l
▷

Spotted Medick
(*Medicago arabica*)

Fields/wasteland/hedgerows
Leguminosae

You can tell this from Black Medick, which is very much like it, by the black spot on each leaflet, and by the seed pods, which are coiled in a spiral, and covered with tiny spines. The flowers are much larger, too, with from one to four in a cluster. It is often found in lawns, as well as meadows and on footpaths.

Annual

Toadflax
(*Linaria vulgaris*)

Fields/wasteland/hedgerows
Scrophulariaceae

The flowers of Toadflax are an interesting shape; they are two-lipped, with an orange spot on the lower one, and have a straight spur at the back 1.5–3 centimetres long. The way the lips are closed together was thought to look like a toad's mouth. The stems grow to about 30–60 centimetres long, with narrow short leaves all the way up and the flowers form a spike, appearing from June to October. **Perennial**

Yellow Archangel
(*Lamiastrum galeobdolon*)

Shady places/woodland
Labiatae

If you know the ordinary white Dead-nettle, you will easily recognize this plant, which is very like it, but with pale golden-yellow flowers in May and June. The hollow stems grow to 20–30 centimetres long and are square; whorls of flowers grow with the pointed, toothed leaves, spaced up the stems. The plant has a distinctive smell. **Perennial**

Yellow Bartsia
(*Parentucellia viscosa*)

Fields/wasteland/hedges
Scrophulariaceae

Not a very common plant, often growing near the sea, or in marshy fields. The whole plant has a sticky feel to it. Stems are 15–45 centimetres tall, the pointed leaves are toothed and in pairs, except in the flower spike, and the flowers are two-lipped, with the upper lip hooded and the lower being three-lobed. Flowering is from June to September. It is a partial parasite. **Annual**

Yellow Corydalis

(Corydalis lutea)

Fields/wasteland/hedgerows
Fumariaceae

This corydalis is a filmy, pretty plant, with delicate stems up to 15–25 centimetres long, and rounded but much divided pale green leaves. Spikes of deep yellow, two-lipped tubular flowers about one centimetre long appear from May to September. It likes stony places and walls. It used to be thought that the smoke from burning the plant would drive away wicked influences. **Perennial**

BELL-SHAPED/OTHERS

Comfrey (Knitbone)

(Symphytum officinale)

Damp places/water
Boraginaceae

Comfrey is quite a large plant, perhaps 90 centimetres tall, with hairy leaves 20 centimetres or more long and broadly lanceolate. The drooping, bell-like flowers appear from May to July, and are generally pale yellow, but on some plants are purple or pinkish. The leaves are said to be very useful as a poultice for broken bones. **Perennial**

Creeping Jenny

(Lysimachia nummularia)

Damp places/water
Primulaceae

This plant has the other common name of Moneywort, perhaps because of the golden flowers, which look like golden coins. It flowers from July to August and likes shady places; the stems lie flat on the ground or hang down over banks or walls, with the round leaves along them in pairs. It was once used for healing wounds. **Perennial**

Daffodil

(Narcissus pseudonarcissus)

Shady places/woodland
Amaryllidaceae

Wild Daffodils are not often seen now, but where they do grow, they are in quite large numbers. They are just like the garden Daffodils, though much shorter, about 20 centimetres tall, and flower at the same time (from March to April). **Perennial**

Green Flowers

Alexanders △
C 50-60mm x

Fat Hen
Fs 100-150mm l
▷

Dock
Fs 130-230mm l
◁

Dog's Mercury
△
F 4-5mm x

Hop
Fh 50mm l (f)
◁

Plantain
Fs 100-150mm l
◁

Moschatel ▽
F 10-15mm l

Nettle
C up to 100mm l
▷

GROUPED FLOWERS

Alexanders
(Smyrnium olusatrum)

Coast/seashore
Umbelliferae

This is a stout, hollow-stemmed plant, about 90 centimetres tall, with yellowish green leaves rather like Celery, and leaflets in threes, each one about 5 centimetres long, and coarsely toothed. Tiny, yellow-green flowers come in umbrella-like clusters in April to June. **Biennial**

Dock
(Rumex obtusifolius)

Fields/wasteland/hedgerows
Polygonaceae

Rubbing dock leaves on nettle stings is supposed to stop the pain and they do contain a substance used to soothe bites and rashes. The leaves are 20–25 centimetres long, with rounded ends, and stems 60–90 centimetres long, with spikes of tiny green flowers turning reddish, in summer. **Perennial**

Dog's Mercury
(Mercurialis perennis)

Shady places/woodland
Euphorbiaceae

Up to 20–30 centimetres tall, downy all over, with pointed, toothed, oblong leaves in pairs, this plant has tiny green flowers in tassels on long stalks in spring. It is named after the Greek god Mercury, who was said to have found it, and the word 'dog' meant that the plant was of no particular use. It is poisonous. **Perennial**

Fat Hen
(Chenopodium album)

Fields/wasteland/hedgerows
Chenopodiaceae

A grey-green plant, though the mealy covering rubs off, to show deep green; up to 60–90 centimetres tall, with diamond-shaped or narrow, toothed leaves, alternate and shortly stalked, it has spikes of tiny, mealy green flowers from July to August. It used to be fed to chickens. **Annual**

Hop
(Humulus lupulus)

Fields/wasteland/hedgerows
Cannabaceae

A tall, climbing plant, twining round supports up to 3 metres and more, with slightly prickly stems, and palmate leaves divided into three lobes, toothed at the edges. The hop or female 'flower' consists of overlapping, light green bracts, in a rounded cone, appearing in August and September. These flowers give beer its bitter taste. **Perennial**

Moschatel
(Adoxa moschatellina)

Shady places/woodland
Adoxaceae

Although easily missed, this is a pretty little plant. The feathery leaves are like Wood Anemone leaves, and the delicate stems 12 centimetres tall, each have five small green flowers, four at right-angles to each other, and one on the top. It is sometimes called Townhall Clock because the four flowers facing outwards are like the faces of a townhall clock. Each flower has four petals; flowering is from March to May. It has a musky perfume. **Perennial**

Nettle
(Urtica dioica)

Shady places/woodland
Urticaceae

The stings and blisters that this plant's leaves cause identify it at once; it grows 60–180 centimetres tall, has toothed, long-triangular pointed leaves in pairs, and drooping tassels of tiny green flowers from June to September. The tiny spines on the leaves contain a juice which, when the spines are broken open, produces the well-known burning feeling. **Perennial**

Plantain
(Plantago major)

Fields/wasteland/hedgerows
Plantaginaceae

Broad, stalked leaves, 10–20 centimetres long, grow in a cluster at the base of the plant, sometimes flat on the ground. Half the stem consists of the green flower spike 10 centimetres long, like a rat's tail, appearing May to September. The plant was once an important medicinal herb, and is still so used. **Perennial**

Twayblade △
F 10-15mm l

Wood Spurge △
C 40-50mm x

Sun Spurge △
C 40-50mm x

Sorrel
Fs 15-40mm l
◁

46

Mignonette
F 6mm x
▷

Black Bryony
F 5mm x
▽

Green Hellebore △
F 20-30mm x

47

Sorrel
(Rumex acetosa)

Fields/wasteland/hedgerows
Chenopodiaceae

Sorrel has stalked arrow-shaped leaves, 7–12 centimetres long, and stems 30–60 centimetres tall. From May to August, spikes of small green flowers appear, later turning red, followed by seed pods with 'wings'. The leaves of the Sorrels can be eaten in salads. **Perennial**

Sun Spurge
(Euphorbia helioscopias)

Fields/wasteland/hedgerows
Euphorbiaceae

The Sun Spurge is a small, yellowish green plant, 15–30 centimetres tall, often a weed in gardens. The stem leaves are oblong, and the leaf-like bracts below the flower clusters are oval; small, lime-green flowers come in stalked clusters from spring to autumn. The stems when cut produce a white juice which is painful on the skin or to the lips and mouth. **Annual**

Twayblade
(Listera ovata)

Shady places/woodland
Orchidaceae

You will find this orchid in flower between May and July. It has a long spike of green flowers, each with a dangling lower petal forked almost in two, and the top petals and sepals forming a kind of rounded hood. The stem is 30–45 centimetres tall, with two broad-oval leaves 10 centimetres long, near the base. *Tway* is from an Anglo-Saxon word meaning two, referring to the forked lower petal. **Perennial**

Wood Spurge
(Euphorbia amygdaloides)

Shady places/woodland
Euphorbiaceae

This Spurge has several tough, almost woody stems 60 centimetres or more tall. Sometimes tinted red, the stem leaves are narrow and alternate. The small, lime-green flowers come in clusters, with two yellowish green, rounded bracts joined at the stem to make one. Flowering time is from March to June. The white juice of this species is as damaging as that of the Sun Spurge. **Perennial**

SIX OR MORE PETALS

Black Bryony
(Tamus communis)

Shady places/woodland
Dioscoreaceae

This is often mistaken for White Bryony, but the leaves of Black Bryony are quite different, as they consist of a single, shiny, heart-shaped, pointed blade on a stalk. The plant climbs by twining, up to about 400 centimetres, and has tiny, six-petalled green-yellow flowers in a loose spike from May to July, followed by round red berries. It is very poisonous.

Perennial

Mignonette
(Reseda lutea)

Fields/wasteland/hedgerows
Resedaceae

About 15–30 centimetres tall, the wild Mignonette has a loose spike of six-petalled, stalked greenish yellow flowers only 6 millimetres or so wide, appearing from June to September. The leaves have a long, narrow, central part, and two, four, or more, long narrow side lobes; sometimes they are long and narrow without lobes. The name comes from the Latin *resedere*, to sedate; the plant smells faintly fragrant.

Biennial

FIVE PETALS

Green Hellebore
(Helleborus viridis)

Shady places/woodland
Ranunculaceae

Clusters of bright green, stalked, drooping flowers appear from February to April, on stems 15–30 centimetres tall. The flowers are pretty, about 2 or 3 centimetres wide, consisting of five pointed, spreading sepals. The palmate leaves are toothed and cut deeply into 7–11 lobes. It is poisonous. *Viridis* is the Latin word for green.

Perennial

Herb Paris
F 30-35mm x

Old Man's Beard
F 15-20mm x
▽

White Bryony
F 10-18mm x

Stinking Hellebore
F 10-30mm x
▽

Wood Sage
F 10mm l
△

Lords and Ladies
Fs up to 50mm l
▷

White Bryony
(Bryonia cretica dioica)

Fields/wasteland/hedgerows
Cucurbitaceae

This belongs to the same plant family as marrows and cucumbers, and has round, pea-sized berries, in autumn, of various colours – yellow, orange, red, or green – depending on ripeness. It climbs in hedges and bushes, and has five-petalled, small green-white flowers in long-stalked clusters all summer. Leaves are five-lobed, palm-shaped, and the plant attaches itself by tendrils. The whole plant is poisonous.   **Perennial**

FOUR PETALS

Herb Paris
(Paris quadrifolia)

Shady places/woodland
Liliaceae

This plant got its name from *par*, meaning equal, because of the regular way in which the four pointed, oval leaves are arranged at the top of the 20–30 centimetres long stems. Flowers are star-like, with eight pointed, green sepals, appearing in May to July, followed by black berries. The plant is poisonous.   **Perennial**

Old Man's Beard
(Clematis vitalba)

Shady places/woodland
Ranunculaceae

In late summer and autumn you will see the grey-white, fluffy, rounded seedheads which give this climbing plant its common name. The woody stems grow to a length of 5 metres or more, attaching by twining the stalks of the 5-parted leaves round suitable supports. The greenish flowers have four pointed sepals, and a large cluster of stamens when they appear in July.   **Perennial**

TWO-LIPPED/PEAFLOWERS

Wood Sage
(Teucrium scorodonia)

Shady places/woodland
Labiatae

The leaves of the Wood Sage are wrinkled and heart-shaped, with rounded teeth. They grow in pairs on a square, reddish stem. The lime-green two-lipped flowers have long purple stamens, and grow in loose branching spikes during July and August. The leaves were once used, like hops, to flavour beer and clear it. **Perennial**

BELL-SHAPED/OTHERS

Lords and Ladies (Cuckoo Pint)
(Arum maculatum)

Shady places/woodland
Araceae

A peculiar-looking wild plant, which has a large, pale green 'leaf' or bract, forming a kind of hood protecting a purple or yellowish finger-like spike of minute flowers, which bloom from March to May. A cluster of red berries follows, growing at the base of the spike. The arrow-shaped leaves are 15 centimetres or more long, and spotted black. It is a poisonous plant, but the roots were once used to provide starch for ruffles in the 16th century. **Perennial**

Stinking Hellebore
(Helleborus foetidus)

Shady places/woodland
Ranunculaceae

Much larger than the Green Hellebore, this one grows up to 30–45 centimetres tall, has simple palmate leaves, somewhat toothed, and many light green, bell-shaped flowers about 2 centimetres wide. The edges of the petal-like sepals are dark red. It flowers from February to March, and is grown in gardens. Its smell is strong and unpleasant. **Perennial**

Blue Flowers

Sea Holly
Fh 20mm x
▽

△
Chicory
Fh 25-40mm x

Sheep's-bit
Fh up to 35mm x
▽

△
Borage
F 20-25mm x

Dog Violet
F 15-25mm x
▽

Flax
F 25mm x
◁

Milkwort
F 3-6mm l
◁

Forget-me-not
F 4mm x
△

Meadow Cranesbill
F 25-30mm x
▽

GROUPED FLOWERS

Chicory
(Cichorium intybus)

Fields/wasteland/hedgerows
Compositae

An angular, stiff plant, whose tough branching stem grows to 45–75 centimetres tall, with leaves rather like those of Dandelion, and sky-blue, daisy-like flowers appearing in small clusters during July and August. The thick, white tap-root is ground, dried and roasted, to be used as a substitute for coffee.

Perennial

Sea Holly
(Eryngium maritimum)

Coasts/sea-shore
Umbelliferae

The tough, stiff, grey-blue leaves have pointed lobes ending in very sharp spines with similarly prickly bracts round the flower heads. The sky-blue flowers appear from June through the summer. It is a bushy plant, about 30 centimetres tall. The roots used to be cooked, candied and eaten as sweets. **Perennial**

Sheep's-bit
(Jasione montana)

Fields/wasteland/hedgerows
Campanulaceae

Quite a common plant, up to about 20–30 centimetres tall, this has a flowerhead like a small Scabious, but blue. If you look closely at a single flower, you will see that it is deeply cut into five narrow, pointed petal lobes. Leaves are narrow and wavy at the edges. It smells disagreeable when bruised; flowering time is from May to September. **Biennial**

FIVE PETALS

Borage
(Borago officinalis)

Fields/wasteland/hedgerows
Boraginaceae

The 30–45 centimetres long flowering stem has drooping clusters of stalked, brilliant blue, star-like flowers, each with five turned-back petals, and a pointed centre of dark stamens. The leaves are large, oblong and roughly hairy. Flowering is between March and November. **Annual**

Dog Violet
(Viola canina)

Fields/wasteland/hedgerows
Violaceae

It grows on sandy soil; the pale, scentless flowers appear from April to June. About 6 centimetres high, its leaves grow alternately, not in clusters as do those of the Wood Violet.

Perennial

Flax
(Linum perenne)

Fields/wasteland/hedgerows
Linaceae

The slender stems grow 30–60 centimetres tall, with narrow, alternate leaves about 2 centimetres long, and blue, 2.5 centimetres wide flowers with five round-tipped petals appearing in June. Flax fibre comes from the cultivated species.

Perennial

Forget-me-not
(Myosotis arvensis)

Fields/wasteland/hedgerows
Boraginaceae

The sky-blue flowers are only about 4 millimetres wide, clustered on hairy, straggling stems about 30 centimetres tall. Flowering time is from April to October. The stem is coiled at first but straightens as the flowers open.

Annual

Meadow Cranesbill
(Geranium pratense)

Fields/wasteland/hedgerows
Geraniaceae

The blue flower petals are veined with purple. Stems are about 30–60 centimetres high, and the leaves are palmate, divided into five or more lobes, very much cut on the edges and with long stalks.

Perennial

Milkwort
(Polygala vulgaris)

Fields/wasteland/hedgerows
Polygalaceae

A small plant, 10 centimetres tall, occasionally taller, with tiny, narrow, alternate leaves, and spikes of shortly stalked, bright blue flowers (sometimes pink or white), 3–6 millimetres long, appearing from May to September. This plant is common on chalky soils.

Perennial

Self-heal
F 10-15mm l
▷

Persian Speedwell
F 12mm x
▽

Bugle
F 10mm x
▽

Periwinkle
F 25-30mm x
◁

Ivy-leaved
Bell-flower
F 3-5mm x
▷

Bluebell
F 12mm l
▷

Harebell
F 15mm l
△

Skullcap
F 6-12mm l
▽

▷
Viper's Bugloss
F 15-20mm x

Periwinkle
Shady places/woodland
Apocynaceae

(Vinca minor)

Tough, trailing stems rooting at the leaf joints, have opposite evergreen oval leaves, 1–2 centimetres long, and single blue flowers with five, joined petals, in spring.   **Perennial**

FOUR PETALS

Persian Speedwell
Damp places/water
Scrophulariaceae

(Veronica persica)

The rapidly growing stems root at the leaf-joints. The ovate leaves are mostly alternate, toothed and about one centimetre wide, and the four-petalled blue flowers, appearing most of the year, grow on long stalks. Each flower is about 1.2 centimetres wide; the lower petal is white. This speedwell grows on damp soils, and flowers most of the year. There are several speed-wells, all with similar flowers but with varying sizes and leaf shapes.   **Annual**

TWO-LIPPED/PEAFLOWERS

Bugle
Shady places/woodland
Labiatae

(Ajuga reptans)

The peculiar common name may be an altered derivation of a Latin word meaning 'to drive away', because it was thought to get rid of various illnesses. A plant with creeping stems rooting at the leaf joints, and paired stalked leaves having rounded teeth, the short flowering spikes of blue, tubular, two-lipped flowers appear in clusters from April to June.   **Perennial**

Self-heal
Fields/wasteland/hedgerows
Labiatae

(Prunella vulgaris)

The blue-purple flowers are all bunched up together in a short spike at the top of each stem. The leaves and stem are often reddish, too, and the leaves are pointed and toothed. Flower-ing time is summer and autumn. Once used for curing throat troubles.   **Perennial**

Skullcap

(Scutellaria galericulata)

Damp places/water
Labiatae

Skullcap has creeping, rooting stems. The paired leaves are somewhat narrow and slightly toothed, and the paired flowers are bright blue with a white throat, about 6–12 millimetres long. The flowering stem is 15–30 centimetres tall, flowering all summer. The capped pod gives the name. **Perennial**

BELL-SHAPED/OTHERS

Bluebell

(Hyacinthoides non-scripta)

Shady places/woodland
Liliaceae

About 30 centimetres tall, the flowering stems with the blue, (sometimes white or pink-lilac) bell-shaped flowers appear in May in woods. The flower stem grows from a bulb, and has long, narrow leaves 15–25 centimetres in length. **Perennial**

Harebell

(Campanula rotundifolia)

Fields/wasteland/hedgerows
Campanulaceae

Between 15 and 30 centimetres tall, the Harebell has slender stems with stalked, rounded leaves low down and long, narrow ones on the stem. The pale blue flowers appear from July to October. **Perennial**

Ivy-leaved Bell-flower

(Wahlenbergia hederacea)

Shady places/woodland
Campanulaceae

A trailing delicate plant with thin stems and ivy-like stalked leaves 2–3 centimetres wide. The bell-like, blue flowers appear in summer and early autumn. The plant is often found on acid moors. **Perennial**

Viper's Bugloss

(Echium vulgare)

Fields/wasteland/hedgerows
Labiatae

It grows at least 60 centimetres tall, and has long, narrow, bristly-hairy leaves, and hairy stems; the flowers open pink and turn bright blue. They are tubular, with five lobes, and are in short spikes appearing from June to August. **Perennial**

Purple Flowers

Creeping Thistle
Fh 15-25mm x (m) (f)
▽

Black Knapweed
Fh 20-40mm x
▽

Burdock
Fh 35-40mm x
△

Field Scabious
Fh 30-40mm x

△
Spear Thistle
Fh 20-40mm x

Ground Thistle
Fh 20-50mm x
▽

△
Teasel
Fh 70mm l

63

GROUPED FLOWERS

Black Knapweed
(Centaurea nigra)

Fields/wasteland/hedgerows
Compositae

The other common name, Hardheads, refers to the distinctive, enlarged, rounded support for the flowers, which is brown-black. The height of Black Knapweed is 30–60 centimetres, its leaves are long and narrow, occasionally toothed, and the purple flowers, rather brush-like, appear from June to September. Mixed with pepper, the roots and seeds were used to improve the appetite. **Perennial**

Burdock
(Arctium lappa)

Fields/wasteland/hedgerows
Compositae

A stout plant up to 120 centimetres tall, with large dock-like leaves, topped by many heads of clustered tiny, tubular purplish flowers (from August to October), nearly hidden by the mass of hooked prickles which form the bur. These get very firmly stuck into the fur or wool of animals, and so the plant is carried and spread a long way from its original home. **Biennial**

Creeping Thistle
(Cirsium arvense)

Fields/wasteland/hedgerows
Compositae

Regarded by many gardeners as a particularly bad weed, this thistle spreads quickly by its creeping white roots. The long lobed leaves are very prickly. The tiny lilac-purple flowers look like a sweep's brush coming out of the flowerhead; the latter is round if male, long if female. Height is 90–120 centimetres, flowering season from July to September. **Perennial**

Field Scabious

(Knautia arvensis)

Fields/wasteland/hedgerows
Dipsacaceae

Once called the Fairies' Pincushion, the lilac-purple flowers of Scabious appear from July to September, on stems 30–60 centimetres tall. The leaves are coarsely pinnate low down, but much more feathery higher up. Scabious mostly grows on chalky soil and in dry, grassy places. **Perennial**

Ground Thistle

(Cirsium acaule)

Fields/wasteland/hedgerows
Compositae

A curious thistle; the reddish purple flowerhead grows without a stem (*acaule* means stemless) in the centre of a cluster of extremely prickly leaves growing straight out of the ground. Look for them in July and August in meadows not cultivated for several years. **Perennial**

Spear Thistle

(Cirsium vulgare)

Fields/wasteland/hedgerows
Compositae

Unlike the other two thistles, this one has a very spiny flowerhead. Dark purple flowers appear from July to September. The leaves are up to 30 centimetres long, narrow and sharply spiny, with stems 90–120 centimetres tall. The flowers can be used to make milk sour. If you look at the undersides of the leaves, you will see that they are covered in a white down. **Biennial**

Teasel

(Dipsacus fullonum)

Fields/wasteland/hedgerows
Dipsacaceae

A tall plant, up to 120–150 centimetres, with prickly stems and leaves. The latter are long and narrow, and die before the flowers appear, which is from July to August. The flowerhead is egg-shaped, about 7 centimetres long, and covered in tiny purple flowers surrounded by a mass of spines. It becomes brown and dry, and lasts through the winter. Teasel heads were once used by cloth workers to comb material so as to raise the nap. **Biennial**

Purple Loosestrife
F 10-15mm x
▷

Stinking Iris
F 80mm x
▽

△
Deadly
Nightshade
F 20mm l

Heart's-ease
F 6-25mm x
▽

Hound's Tongue
F 6mm x
▽

Wood Violet
F 12-18mm x
▷

Woody Nightshade ▽
F 15mm x

△
Sea Lavender
F 5mm l

67

SIX OR MORE PETALS

Purple Loosestrife
(Lythrum salicaria)

Damp places/water
Lythraceae

The bright purple flowers in long spikes have six petals and prominent stamens; they appear between June and October. Height is 60–90 centimetres, the stems reddish, with leaves like those of Willow. **Perennial**

Stinking Iris
(Iris foetidissima)

Shady places/woodland
Iridaceae

The long, narrow, pointed, bad-smelling leaves surround a flower stem about 60–90 centimetres tall, topped by two or three six-petalled flowers, pale lilac-mauve (very occasionally pale yellow) from May to July. Round, bright red-orange seeds in a 5-centimetre long seed case follow them. The seed case splits open later in the summer. **Perennial**

FIVE PETALS

Deadly Nightshade
(Atropa belladonna)

Fields/wasteland/hedgerows
Solanaceae

This is a very poisonous plant and you should not even handle it. Stems grow to 60–200 centimetres tall, stalked leaves are dark green, ovate and pointed. The five-lobed flowers are bell-shaped, 2 centimetres long, coloured dingy purple with a green tint, appearing from July to September and followed by black shiny, pea-sized berries. **Perennial**

Heart's-ease (Wild Pansy)
(Viola tricolor)

Fields/wasteland/hedgerows
Violaceae

They look like tiny Pansies, and can have the upper petals purple and the lower one yellow or white, but they may also be all purple or all yellow. It grows 10–20 centimetres tall, and the flowers are 6–25 millimetres wide, appearing spring and summer. It was thought to cure heart troubles. **Annual**

Hound's Tongue
(Cynoglossum officinale)

Fields/wasteland/hedgerows
Boraginaceae

A rough bristly plant, 30–60 centimetres tall, it has narrow leaves up to 25 centimetres long, and stalked, purplish red, five-lobed flowers in long clusters from June to August. The plant smells of mice. **Biennial**

Sea Lavender
(Limonium vulgare)

Coast/seashore
Plumbaginaceae

Small, deep purple-blue, unscented flowers are arranged on one side of the top of the stem. They feel dry and papery, and last many weeks after picking, so are called 'Everlastings'. Stem height is 15–45 centimetres, leaves are oblong, up to 15 centimetres, and the flowering time is from July to September. **Perennial**

Wood Violet
(Viola reichenbachiana)

Shady places/woodland
Violaceae

This pale blue-purple unscented violet often grows on hedge banks. It flowers from April to May. The leaves are heart-shaped, with rounded teeth. **Perennial**

Woody Nightshade
(Solanum dulcamara)

Shady places/woodland
Solanaceae

The long trailing stems are tough and woody at the base. The five-petalled flowers seen from June to August are deep purple with bright yellow centres (stamens) and are followed by poisonous green berries changing to yellow and finally red. All parts of the plant are poisonous. **Perennial**

△
Basil Thyme
F 3mm x

△
Thyme
F 4mm x

△
Wild Basil
F 6mm x

△
Marjoram
F 3mm x

70

Betony
F 10mm l

Broomrape
F 10-18mm x

Bush Vetch
F 12-15mm l

Broad-leaved
Helleborine
F 20mm x

Butterwort
F 10-15mm l

FOUR PETALS/TWO-LIPPED FLOWERS

Basil Thyme
(Acinos arvensis)

Fields/wasteland/hedgerows
Labiatae

This is rather an eye-catching little flower, though it is only about 3 millimetres wide; it is deep violet with a white 'face', in clusters, flowering from August to September. The 15 centimetre tall stems carry oval pointed leaves in pairs and the plant is aromatic. It was formerly said to 'drive serpents away'.

Annual

Marjoram
(Origanum vulgare)

Fields/wasteland/hedgerows
Labiatae

The leaves of this herb are still used regularly for cooking, since they have a strong aromatic flavour. The wiry stems grow to 30–45 centimetres, and the oval leaves, 2 centimetres or more long, come in pairs. The tiny flowers are purple-pink, but maroon in bud, and appear in clusters on long stems, at the top of the main stem, from August to September. The leaves are slightly hairy.

Perennial

Thyme
(Thymus serpyllum)

Fields/wasteland/hedgerows
Labiatae

The strong-smelling leaves of Thyme are used a great deal in cooking, especially with meat. It is a small shrub, 15–25 centimetres tall, with woody stems, 6-millimetre long evergreen leaves, and has tiny pale purple flowers in clusters from July to September. It grows in dry places.

Perennial

Wild Basil (Cushion Calamint)
(Clinopodium vulgare)

Fields/wasteland/hedgerows
Labiatae

A softly hairy plant about 30–45 centimetres tall, with paired egg-shaped leaves, 2–5 centimetres long, on square stems. Small, pink-purple tubular flowers with two lips grow in clusters just above the upper leaves, from July to September. The aromatic leaves were once used to make a drink which helped with indigestion.

Perennial

TWO-LIPPED/PEAFLOWERS

Betony
(Betonica officinalis)

Shady places/woodland
Labiatae

Betony is about 30 centimetres tall, and the oblong leaves have rounded teeth and grow in pairs along the square stem. The two-lipped tubular flowers are red-purple, in a dense spike, appearing from June to October. **Perennial**

Broad-leaved Helleborine
(Epipactis helleborine)

Shady places/woodland
Orchidaceae

It is 60–90 centimetres tall; its leaves are broad-ovate with parallel veins, and alternate. The flowers are purple to green with two pointed petals above, and one beneath, in a one-sided spike appearing from July to September. **Perennial**

Broomrape
(Orobanche minor)

Fields/wasteland/hedgerows
Orobanchaceae

This parasite lives on plants of the pea and daisy families. The stem is fleshy, 15–23 centimetres long, beige to yellow, tinted purplish; the flowers are purplish, but may be purplish yellow or red, growing in a spike, from June to September. **Annual**

Bush Vetch
(Vicia sepium)

Fields/wasteland/hedgerows
Leguminosae

This climbs up other plants. Pinnate leaves have three to nine pairs of leaflets and purple-blue flowers are in short spikes of up to six, in summer, followed by 2.5 centimetre long black pods. **Perennial**

Butterwort
(Pinguicula vulgaris)

Damp places/water
Lentibulariaceae

The oblong leaves, which form a basal rosette, roll inwards and trap insects. The flowers, which come singly at the top of 15 centimetres long stems, are blue-purple with five lobes and a long spur. Look for them in May and June. **Perennial**

Tufted Vetch
F 10-12mm I
◁

Ground Ivy
F 20mm J
◁

Early Purple Orchid
Fs 70-150mm I
▷

Figwort
F 10mm x
△

△
Purple Dead-nettle
F 10-15mm I

Wood Woundwort
F 14mm x

Bell Heather
F 6mm l

Vetch
F 10-30mm l

Foxglove
F 40-50mm l

Early Purple Orchid

Shady places/woodland
Orchidaceae

(Orchis mascula)

The purple two-lipped flowers have a long spur, and the lower lip has three lobes; they are in a loose spike 7–15 centimetres long. The entire stem is 15–30 centimetres high, and the leaves are narrow, blotched and spotted with black. The plant flowers from April to June and grows in damp soil.   **Perennial**

Figwort

Shady places/woodland
Scrophulariaceae

(Scrophularia nodosa)

A coarse plant, 60–90 centimetres tall, having a four-cornered stem, and large ovate leaves with pointed teeth, in pairs. The purplish-brown, rounded flowers are two-lipped, with all-green sepals, and appear from June to September. **Perennial**

Ground Ivy

Fields/wasteland/hedgerows
Labiatae

(Glechoma hederacea)

This is a small, creeping evergreen plant with quite long stems, stalked rounded leaves in pairs with rounded teeth, and purple-blue tubular flowers 2 centimetres long, with five lobes, appearing in spring.   **Perennial**

Purple Dead-nettle

Fields/wasteland/hedgerows
Labiatae

(Lamium purpureum)

The toothed and pointed (or rounded) leaves grow, like those of Nettle, in pairs, with stalks, along stems 15–30 centimetres tall. Small pink-purple tubular flowers, which have an upper hood and a lower lip, appear in spring and summer. The leaves do not sting.   **Annual**

Tufted Vetch

Fields/wasteland/hedgerows
Leguminosae

(Vicia cracca)

Up to 60–90 centimetres tall, this climbs up other plants. Its purple-blue flowers form a one-sided spike of up to 40 flowers, from June until August, and each leaf has 9–12 pairs of leaflets. The seed pods are brown.   **Perennial**

Vetch
(Vicia sativa)

Fields/wasteland/hedgerows
Leguminosae

The commonest vetch, growing 30–60 centimetres tall. The feathery leaves have between four and seven pairs of leaflets and end in tendrils; the red- or blue-purple peaflowers are in pairs, appearing from April to August. *Sativa* is the Latin word for cultivated; this is a wild plant grown as cattle food.

Annual

Wood Woundwort
(Stachys sylvatica)

Fields/wasteland/hedgerows
Labiatae

This grows at least 60 centimetres tall. It is hairy and smells strongly and unpleasantly when trodden on. The leaves are pointed-ovate and toothed; the flowers are dark reddish purple in clusters of about six up the stem, appearing from July to September. It is good for stopping bleeding. **Perennial**

BELL-SHAPED/OTHERS

Bell Heather
(Erica cinerea)

High places/mountains
Ericaceae

You will find this plant on moors and heaths, quite high up. It has tough woody stems, and grows into a little bush, about 30 centimetres tall. The tiny evergreen leaves are very narrow and pointed, in clusters of three to four. Bell-shaped, reddish purple flowers one millimetre long grow in short spikes from July to September. **Perennial**

Foxglove
(Digitalis purpurea)

Shady places/woodland
Scrophulariaceae

One of the prettiest of the wild flowers, the purple and white spotted bells of the Foxglove appear in spikes from June to September. Stems are 90–180 centimetres tall and the leaves are 30 centimetres long, mainly in a rosette at the base. The Latin *digitus* means finger; fox was originally 'folks', that is the fairies, so Foxgloves were once thought to be the gloves of the fairies. **Biennial**

Lilac Flowers

Winter Heliotrope
Fs 15mm x

Corn Mint
F 2mm x

Water Mint
C 30mm x

Pennyroyal
C 15mm x

Lady's Smock
F 12-20mm x
◁

Sea Stock
F 30mm x
▷

Sea Rocket
F 20mm x
▽

79

GROUPED FLOWERS

Corn Mint
(Mentha arvensis)

Damp places/water
Labiatae

The mint used in mint sauce is related to the Corn Mint, whose leaves are also aromatic, but rather unpleasantly. Height is 15–30 centimetres, the whole plant being softly hairy; the oval, paired leaves have rounded teeth, and the upper ones have a cluster of tiny lilac flowers just above them, except for the very top leaves. Flowering time is from July to September, and it likes rather damp meadows. **Perennial**

Pennyroyal
(Mentha pulegium)

Damp places/water
Labiatae

Quite different in habit, this mint has creeping stems, rooting at the leaf-joints, and so forms a mat of shoots. The leaves are about one centimetre long, and lilac flowers grow in clusters along the stems, from July to October. Its strong flavour makes it unpopular for cooking nowadays. **Perennial**

Water Mint
(Mentha aquatica)

Damp places/water
Labiatae

You will find this growing beside streams or ponds, even actually in shallow water. It has the strong smell characteristic of all this genus. The plant is hairy and tinged purplish, with round-toothed leaves in pairs, and grows 30–45 centimetres tall. Stems end in a rounded head of pinkish lilac flowers, appearing in August and September. **Perennial**

Winter Heliotrope
(Petasites fragrans)

Fields/wasteland/hedgerows
Compositae

The lilac, brush-like almond-scented flowers in short spikes appear in January on fleshy stems 15–30 centimetres tall. The leaves are 15 centimetres wide, rounded and toothed; they are white-woolly on the underside, appearing when the flowers have died. Winter Heliotrope grows in damp soils. **Perennial**

FOUR PETALS

Lady's Smock
(Cardamine pratensis)

Fields/wasteland/hedgerows
Cruciferae

An alternative name is the Cuckoo Flower, as it flowers from April to May when the cuckoo is heard, or sometimes Milkmaids. It grows profusely in damp meadows, and is about 30 centimetres tall; the basal leaves are feathery, with rounded leaflets, and the stalked four-petalled flowers are lilac coloured, a few in a cluster. The leaves taste peppery and were once added to salads. **Perennial**

Sea Rocket
(Cakile maritima)

Coast/seashore
Cruciferae

This grows right by the sea, out of the sand or shingle on the beach. Greyish green all over, the stems grow up to about 30 centimetres long, and the fleshy leaves are pinnate. Lilac, four-petalled flowers in a short spike appear from June to August, followed by egg-shaped pointed pods. *Cakile* is an Arabic word; one species grows in Arabian deserts. **Annual**

Sea Stock
(Matthiola sinuata)

Coast/seashore
Cruciferae

Sea Stock is a bushy little plant, about 30 centimetres tall, completely covered in a soft white woolly down, making the leaves and stems grey-green. The lower leaves are wavy edged or slightly lobed; all are narrow. The flowers are four-petalled, lilac, and strongly scented at night, appearing from May to July. It grows on sandy coasts. **Biennial**

Pink Flowers

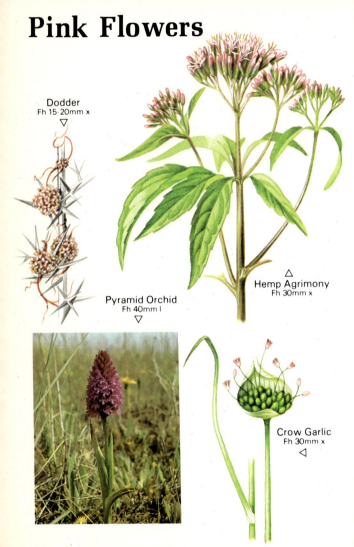

Dodder
Fh 15-20mm x
▽

Hemp Agrimony
Fh 30mm x
△

Pyramid Orchid
Fh 40mm l
▽

Crow Garlic
Fh 30mm x
◁

Red Clover △
Fh 30mm x

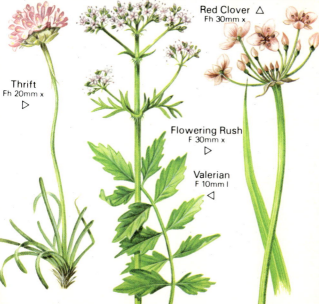

Thrift
Fh 20mm x
▷

Flowering Rush
F 30mm x
▷

Valerian
F 10mm l
◁

GROUPED FLOWERS

Crow Garlic
(Allium vineale)

Fields/wasteland/hedgerows
Liliaceae

Small pink, bell-shaped flowers on long stalks are mixed up with tiny bulbs in the flowerhead, which has a white papery sheath round it, and tops a stem 30 centimetres long. Crow Garlic flowers from June to August. The leaves are tubular; and each plant has many bulbs lying below the ground.

Perennial

Dodder
(Cuscuta epithymum)

Fields/wasteland/hedgerows
Convolvulaceae

You will probably find the unpleasant smelling Dodder twined round the Gorse's stems. It looks like reddish pink netting, and the pink flowers are in round clusters along the stems from July to September. It is a parasite, and also grows on heather.

Annual

Hemp Agrimony
(Eupatorium cannabinum)

Damp places/water
Compositae

Found in marshes, ditches and beside streams, the Hemp Agrimony grows up to 60–150 centimetres tall, with reddish, downy stems. When cut, they give off a pleasant smell. The leaves are narrow, pointed and palmate, with toothed edges; the small flowers are pink-purple and tubular, growing in thick, flat-topped clusters from July to September.

Perennial

Pyramid Orchid
(Anacamptis pyramidalis)

Fields/wasteland/hedgerows
Orchidaceae

The shape of the flowerhead gives this orchid its common name, since the flower spike is stunted and contracted into a pyramid. The pink or pink-purple flowers each have a three-lobed, flattened lip, and a long, thin, curved spur. The plant flowers all summer from June; height is up to 30 centimetres and leaves are narrow and pointed.

Perennial

Red Clover
(Trifolium pratense)

Fields/wasteland/hedgerows
Leguminosae

Clover is still associated with good luck, as is Shamrock *(Trifolium repens)*. It is a low creeping plant, with white blotches on the leaves, and pink flowerheads, from May to October. A very popular plant with bees, honey made from it has a delicious flavour. Farmers sow it mixed with grass in fields as grazing for cows. **Perennial**

Thrift
(Armeria maritima)

Coast/seashore
Plumbaginaceae

This forms dark green cushions of short, thread-like leaves, like fine grass, with flowering stems 10–20 centimetres tall growing up from them. Round flowerheads of tiny five-lobed pink flowers appear any time from April to August. Look for it on cliffs, rocks and in gardens. **Perennial**

Valerian
(Valeriana officinalis)

Damp places/water (also dry hills)
Valerianaceae

A dark green-leaved plant up to 60–120 centimetres tall, with the lower part of the stem hairy. The leaves are feathery, with toothed narrow leaflets. Round clusters of small, pale pink flowers appear from June to August. The dried root has been used in medicine for many centuries; it was also used to perfume clothes and sheets. **Perennial**

SIX OR MORE PETALS

Flowering Rush
(Butomus umbellatus)

Damp places/water
Butomaceae

This plant grows directly out of the water, and flowers from July to September. Height is 60–120 centimetres, with narrow, triangular, sharp-edged leaves, and a thick hollow stem, topped by a cluster of long-stalked, bright pink, six-petalled flowers. It has purple, egg-shaped seed pods. The generic name comes from two Greek words meaning 'mouth' and 'to cut'. **Perennial**

Bogbean
F 15mm x
▽

Centaury
F 7mm x
◁

Dog Rose
F 45-50mm x
▽

Herb Robert
F 20mm x
▽

△
Mallow
F 25-40mm x

Red Campion
F 18-25mm x
▷

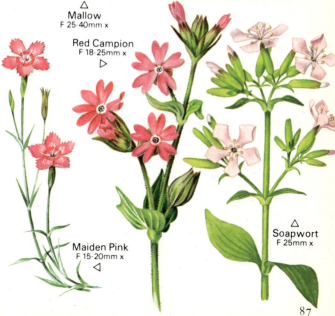

Maiden Pink
F 15-20mm x
◁

△
Soapwort
F 25mm x

FIVE PETALS

Bogbean
(Menyanthes trifoliata)

Damp places/water
Menyanthaceae

The fringed pink tubular flowers of the Bogbean appear during spring and early summer in short spikes above the water; it is an aquatic plant. The leaves, in three parts, also grow well above the water and are like those of the vegetable Broad Bean. They were once used medicinally and contain vitamin C. **Perennial**

Centaury
(Centaurium erythraea)

Fields/wasteland/hedgerows
Gentianaceae

A short plant about 15 centimetres tall, but it can be much shorter or much taller. It has ovate leaves, mostly at the base in a rosette and the clustered pink flowers are tubular, with five lobes. It flowers between June and September. It is still used for making a drink called vermouth. **Annual/biennial**

Dog Rose
(Rosa canina)

Fields/wasteland/hedgerows
Rosaceae

A wild rose with unscented leaves and fragrant flowers, sometimes white instead of pink. The leaves have four to six leaflets, and there are only a few thorns on the stems. Flowering time is July. *Canina* is the specific name because it was thought that the plant cured rabies resulting from a dog's bite. **Perennial**

Herb Robert
(Geranium robertianum)

Shady places/woodland
Geraniaceae

The reddish, hairy, branched stems of this plant grow to about 30 centimetres tall and, being brittle, break easily. The triangular leaves have two or three pinnate leaflets, and the deep pink flowers have five petals. The whole plant has a strong and not very pleasant smell; flowering time is from April to November. The reason for the common name may be to do with St Robert. **Annual/biennial**

Maiden Pink

(Dianthus deltoides)

Fields/wasteland/hedgerows
Caryophyllaceae

Where this grows, there is a lot of it, but the patches themselves are not very common; it is usually found in sandy places. Stems are 15–30 centimetres high, the leaves stiff, narrow and pointed, about one centimetre long. The solitary deep pink five-petalled flowers, fringed at the petal ends, appear from June to September. The generic name comes from *dios*, divine, and *anthos*, flower, both Greek words.

Perennial

Mallow

(Malva sylvestris)

Fields/wasteland/hedgerows
Malvaceae

The Common Mallow grows up to 90 or 120 centimetres high, with hairy stems, and triangular toothed leaves, 5 centimetres wide, the lobes of which are pleated. The wide-open flowers have five pink-purple petals, narrowed at their base and notched at the opposite end, in bloom from June to September. Seed pods are round, flat on the back, but ribbed on top.

Annual/perennial

Red Campion

(Silene dioica)

Shady places/woodland
Caryophyllaceae

Up to 30–60 centimetres tall, this Campion has longish, pointed leaves in pairs. The rose-pink flowers with five petals, each deeply lobed, come in long-stalked clusters from spring all through summer. *Silene* comes from a Greek word meaning saliva, and refers to the stickiness of the plant. **Biennial**

Soapwort (Bouncing Bet)

(Saponaria officinalis)

Fields/wasteland/hedgerows
Caryophyllaceae

If the leaves and roots are boiled, the resulting liquid contains a kind of soap which will clean clothes, particularly wool; rub the liquid between your hands and it will lather. Clusters of pink flowers rather like Phlox, with five narrow petals, bloom between June and September on stems 30–60 centimetres long. The ovate leaves are 7–10 centimetres long. **Perennial**

Sweet Briar
F 30-40mm x
▽

Ragged Robin
F 30-40mm x
▽

Rosebay Willowherb
F 20-30mm x
▽

△
Tree Mallow
F 50mm x

Balsam
F 30mm l
▽

Fumitory
F 7-9mm l
▽

Water Plantain
F 8-10mm x
▽

Sweet Briar

(Rosa rubiginosa)

Fields/wasteland/hedgerows
Rosaceae

A sweet apple-like scent comes from the leaves of this rose when rubbed, but you will be able to smell it after rain without doing this. A bushy, woody plant up to 90–120 centimetres tall, with five to seven rounded-oval leaflets, stems with hooked prickles and pink flowers in July. **Perennial**

Tree Mallow

(Lavatera arborea)

Fields/wasteland/hedgerows
Malvaceae

A stout upright plant up to 180 centimetres tall with a downy stem, woody lower down. The flowers are pink-purple, and veined purple, in clusters; each is saucer-like with overlapping petals. The blue-green leaves are lobed and are hardly toothed; they feel velvety and were once used for soothing sprains. Tree Mallow mostly grows near the sea and flowers from July to September. **Biennial**

FOUR PETALS

Ragged Robin

(Lychnis flos-cuculae)

Damp places/water
Caryophyllaceae

A 30–60 centimetres tall plant with a few narrow, pointed leaves, and pink, five-petalled flowers appearing from May to June. Each petal is so deeply cut into four lobes as to appear to be torn. **Perennial**

Rosebay Willowherb

(Epilobium angustifolium)

Fields/wasteland/hedgerows
Onagraceae

Sometimes also called Fireweed, because it grows plentifully on ground that has been burnt. Tall, up to 90–120 centimetres, with narrow, willow-like leaves and loose spikes of deep pink-purple, four-petalled flowers appearing from July to September. The seed pods are long and narrow, bursting open to produce fluffy-stemmed seeds. **Annual**

THREE PETALS

Water Plantain
(*Alisma plantago-aquatica*)

Damp places/water
Alismataceae

The Plantain grows in shallow water, such as ditches and edges of ponds; it is 30–90 centimetres tall, with small, pinkish white, three-petalled flowers in long-stalked clusters, from July to August. The leaves grow at the base of the stem, and are ovate to long and narrow. Another of its common names is Mad-dog Weed. **Perennial**

TWO-LIPPED/PEAFLOWERS

Balsam
(*Impatiens glandulifera*)

Damp places/water
Balsaminaceae

This Balsam actually comes from the Himalayas, but has naturalized well enough to grow wild now in Britain. Tall, up to 120–180 centimetres, it has fleshy red-tinted stems and pointed, ovate, toothed leaves, in pairs or threes. Very attractive purplish pink flowers 3 centimetres long, with a large lower lip, and a puffed up spur bent into a little crook at the end, appear from July to October. **Annual**

Fumitory
(*Fumitaria officinalis*)

Fields/wasteland/hedges
Fumariaceae

A delicate and pretty plant, with stems 30 centimetres or more long, trailing or straggling along the ground or up into other plants. Leaves filmy, each with three leaflets lobed and cut; the pink tubular flowers are tipped dark purple, and come in clusters from May to October. They produce a yellow dye, once used for wool. **Annual**

Marsh Helleborine
F 12-20mm x
▽

△
Rest Harrow
F 10-15mm x

Sainfoin
F 12mm l
◁

Lousewort
F 20-25mm l
◁

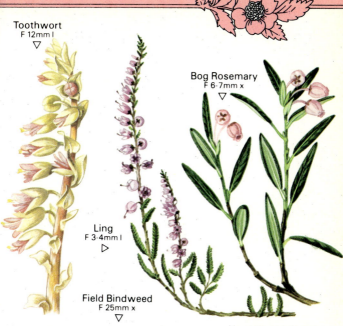

Toothwort
F 12mm l
▽

Bog Rosemary
F 6-7mm x
▽

Ling
F 3-4mm l
▽

Field Bindweed
F 25mm x
▽

Lousewort
(Pedicularis sylvatica)

Fields/wasteland/hedgerows
Scrophulariaceae

A small plant, up to 15 centimetres tall, with pinnate leaves whose segments are widely spaced, and deep pink flowers with a pronounced hood, a lobed lower lip, and a long tube. They can be seen on heaths and hilly fields from April to July. It gets the common name from the idea that sheep eating it become covered in lice, as a result. **Perennial**

Marsh Helleborine
l:pipactis palustris)

Damp places/water
Orchidaceae

Quite large for an orchid, the stem grows to about 30 or 45 centimetres long, and the flowers come on one side of the stem, in a loose spike. The colour varies a lot, but is usually pinkish, with the outer petal-like sepals having a green tint. The lip has yellow spots and is frilled at the edge. Flowering is from June to August. **Perennial**

Rest Harrow
(Ononis repens)

Fields/wasteland/hedgerows
Leguminosae

Often found in fields near the sea, this is a short, semi-shrubby plant with small pink peaflowers, appearing singly or in clusters from July to September. The leaflets are oblong, sometimes in threes. Stems are hairy and occasionally end in a thorn. This plant obtained its common name because the roots are so matted that they stop the plough or harrow from working. **Perennial**

Sainfoin
(Onobrychis vicifolia)

Fields/wasteland/hedgerows
Leguminosae

A plant with several stems 30–45 centimetres tall, with feathery leaves, each with seven or more pairs of leaflets, and pink peaflowers, with darker veins, appearing in a pyramidal spike from June to August. Sainfoin comes from the French words, *sain*, wholesome, and *foin*, hay; the plant is a farm crop for cows and other animals. Sainfoin prefers chalky soil.
Perennial

Toothwort
(Lathraea squamaria)

A parasite, growing under Hazel bushes, from their roots. It has no green colouring, but is a creamy pinkish-coloured, short fleshy plant, about 10 or 15 centimetres tall, with pale pink flowers in a nodding one-sided spike; it flowers from April to May. It grows on the roots of other trees as well as Hazel. **Perennial**

BELL-SHAPED/OTHERS

Bog Rosemary
(Andromeda polifolia)

High places/mountains
Ericaceae

Wet heaths and moors are the home of this small evergreen shrub, which is usually 15–30 centimetres tall. Hanging pink, bell flowers, in clusters at the end of shoots, flower all summer from June. The grey-green leaves are very narrow, and 2.5 centimetres long. **Perennial**

Field Bindweed
(Convolvulus arvensis)

Fields/wasteland/hedgerows
Convolvulaceae

Although this is a climbing plant, it mostly grows along the ground in cornfields and on footpaths. It has pink, open, trumpet-shaped flowers about 2.5 centimetres wide from June to August. The leaves are distinctly arrow-shaped. The bruised flowers will turn clear water yellow or orange.

Perennial

Ling
(Calluna vulgaris)

High places/mountains
Ericaceae

Also called heather, the difference between Ling and the true heathers (*Erica* species) is that the pink flowers are cut into four petal-like segments, and are not true bells. The evergreen leaves are minute, close against the much-branched stems which are 15–30 centimetres tall. It flowers from August to September. *Calluna* comes from the Greek for 'to clean'; Ling was once used for brooms. **Perennial**

White Flowers

Fool's Parsley
C 30mm x

Cow Parsley
C up to 60mm x

Feverfew
Fh 10-25mm x

Daisy
Fh up to 25mm x

Hogweed
C up to 160mm x
▷

△
Hemlock
C 60mm x

Lovage
C 40mm x
▽

Ground Elder
C 40mm x
◁

GROUPED FLOWERS

Cow Parsley
(Anthriscus sylvestris)

Shady places/woodland
Umbelliferae

The tiny white flowers are in clusters on stems (like the ribs of an umbrella), and bloom between April and May, sometimes in March. Height is 60–90 centimetres, with large, very fern-like leaves up to 30 centimetres long. The stems have a strong, not unpleasant smell when broken. **Perennial**

Daisy
(Bellis perennis)

Fields/wasteland/hedgerows
Compositae

Flower stems are up to 5 centimetres tall. Sometimes a plant has pink tips to the petals, or twice as many petals. It flowers from March to October, but all year in mild weather. The name comes from two Saxon words meaning 'day's eye'; the flowers open and shut with daylight. **Perennial**

Feverfew (Featherfew)
(Tanacetum parthenium)

Fields/wasteland/hedgerows
Compositae

The clustered, daisy-like flowers are on top of stems 45–60 centimetres long, and appear from May to September. The leaves are about 11 centimetres long and 5 centimetres wide, somewhat pinnate and toothed, and the whole plant has a strong and rather unpleasant smell. **Perennial**

Fool's Parsley
(Aethusa cynapium)

Fields/wasteland/hedgerows
Umbelliferae

The leaves do look like those of wild parsley, though bigger and less curled. The flowering stem is 30–60 centimetres tall, with tiny white flowers in the umbrella clusters typical of this plant family; they appear from June to October. Beneath the flowers there are long green 'whiskers' (bracts). Do not eat this poisonous plant. **Annual**

Ground Elder (Goutweed)

(*Aegopodium podagraria*)

Fields/wasteland/hedgerows
Umbelliferae

Most often it is only the leaves of this plant which are seen. It flowers late in summer (around August), but the flowering stems are rather sparse. Leaves form a carpet, on stalks about 15 centimetres tall, and have two or three groups of three leaflets, toothed at the edges. The stout, hollow flowering stems are 30–60 centimetres tall, topped by clusters of tiny white flowers from July to August. It was once used to cure stiffness in joints. **Perennial**

Hemlock

(*Conium maculatum*)

Damp places/water
Umbelliferae

Hemlock is an extremely poisonous plant, so do not eat any of it. Leaves are dark green, feathery, large, up to 60 centimetres long. The plant is tall, up to 150 centimetres or more, stems dark red or purple-spotted. Tiny white flowers in umbrella-like clusters appear from July to August. The whole plant smells unpleasant, like mice, especially if bruised. **Biennial**

Hogweed

(*Heracleum sphondylium*)

Shady places/woodland
Umbelliferae

An extremely tall plant, 150–210 centimetres tall, generally hairy, with a stout, hollow stem. The leaves consist of one to three pairs of broad leaflets, each 5–7 centimetres wide, much cut and toothed. The outer petals of the white flowers are much larger than the inner ones, and are deeply lobed, appearing from July to November. **Perennial**

Lovage

(*Ligisticum scoticum*)

Coast/seashore
Umbelliferae

Lovage is a herb whose celery-flavoured leaves are still used for cooking. They are shiny, dark green and made up of groups of three, toothed leaflets. The hollow stem, 120 centimetres or more tall, is tinged purple, and has a cluster of tiny white or yellowish-white flowers in July. Lovage is mostly found in northern Britain. **Perennial**

Meadowsweet
C 70mm x
▷

Pennywort
F 4-10mm l
▽

Ox-eye Daisy
Fh 25-50mm x
▷

Ramsons
C 50mm x
▽

Samphire
C 30-50mm x
▷

Sweet Woodruff
C 12-28mm x
▷

Sweet Cicely
C 30-60mm x
▽

Sneezewort
F 10mm x
△

Sanicle
C 7-20mm x
△

Meadowsweet
(Filipendula ulmaria)

Fields/wasteland/hedgerows
Rosaceae

From June to September, grassy roadsides and meadows left uncut will certainly have Meadowsweet in flower in them; the fluffy clusters of tiny, creamy white, fragrant flowers grow on stems 60–120 centimetres tall. The pinnate, dark green leaves have toothed leaflets, five pairs or less on the lower leaves. Once called *Spiraea ulmaria*, it gave its name to aspirin, the basis of which originally came from the flower-buds.

Perennial

Ox-eye Daisy
(Leucanthemum vulgare)

Fields/wasteland/hedgerows
Compositae

In some meadows, you will see this large daisy in sheets of white from May to September; it is very common and grows by hedges, footpaths and roadsides as well. Height is about 30–60 centimetres; the dark green leaves are ovate or narrow, and toothed. The stem is tough and strong-smelling. *Leucanthemum* comes from the Greek, *leucos*, white.

Perennial

Pennywort
(Umbilicus rupestris)

Fields/wasteland/hedgerows
Crassulaceae

The favourite place for this to grow is out of walls and from between rocks. It has almost completely round, thick, shiny leaves, with a dimple in the middle, on thick 15–30 centimetre long stems, and a spike of white, sometimes greenish white, bell flowers, from June to August. *Rupestris* is a Latin word meaning 'rock-loving'.

Perennial

Ramsons
(Allium ursinum)

Shady places/woodland
Liliaceae

It is not surprising that this has a very strong smell of a bitter kind of garlic, as it is a member of the Onion family. It grows in clumps, and has broad-oval pointed leaves like those of Lily of the Valley. Small white flowers in round heads appear between April and June, on stems 25 centimetres tall.

Perennial

Samphire
(Crithmum maritimum)

Coast/seashore
Umbelliferae

This fleshy aromatic plant is much branched, growing about 30 centimetres tall on sea-splashed rocks. The thick leaves are in three parts and each reduced to narrow segments about 2 centimetres long. Flat-topped clusters of tiny yellow-white flowers appear from July to September. **Perennial**

Sanicle
(Sanicula europaea)

Shady places/woodland
Umbelliferae

The stem is 30–45 centimetres tall, often tinted red, the leaves palmate with three or five toothed lobes, and long stalks. In May to August tiny greenish white flowers (sometimes tinted pink) appear in tight round clusters. **Perennial**

Sneezewort
(Achillea ptarmica)

Fields/wasteland/hedgerows
Compositae

The stem is 30–60 centimetres tall, the leaves narrow, pointed and toothed, and the stalked white flowers are one centimetre wide, in a loose cluster; each flower has 10–15 petals and appears between July and September. Sneezewort grows in damp meadows. **Perennial**

Sweet Cicely
(Myrrhis odorata)

Fields/wasteland/hedgerows
Umbelliferae

This smells of aniseed and grows up to 60–90 centimetres, with a hollow, ribbed stem, and large fern-like leaves. The tiny, white flowers, in a flat-topped head, are followed by 2.5 centimetre seeds. It flowers from May to June. **Perennial**

Sweet Woodruff
(Galium odoratum)

Shady places/woodland
Rubiaceae

The slender stems grow 15–30 centimetres tall, with clusters of about eight narrow leaves spaced up the stem, and tiny white tubular flowers appear in a head at the top from April to June. The dried leaves smell of newly-mown hay. **Perennial**

△
Yarrow
C up to 80mm x

△
Wild Carrot
C 120mm x

△
Wild Angelica
C 50-110mm x

White Clover
Fh 30mm x
◁

Wild Chamomile
Fh 15-40mm x
▽

Black Nightshade
F 8mm x
▽

△
Wood Anemone
F 20-40mm x

Waterlily
F 50-200mm x
▽

Yarrow
(Achillea millefolium)

Fields/wasteland/hedgerows
Compositae

A cultivated form of this is grown in gardens; the wild Yarrow is about 30 centimetres tall, and has dark green, oblong, extremely feathery leaves. Tiny white flowers, sometimes tinged pink, grow in flat-topped clusters from June to August. It has a strong aromatic smell. **Perennial**

White Clover
(Trifolium repens)

Fields/wasteland/hedgerows
Leguminosae

Sometimes called Dutch Clover, the difference between this and Red Clover is that, although the flowers may be pink instead of the normal white, the leaflets are rounded instead of pointed, and slightly toothed. It flowers all summer, and is often grown, mixed with grasses, for grazing farm animals. **Perennial**

Wild Angelica
(Angelica sylvestris)

Shady places/woodland
Umbelliferae

The young stems of the cultivated species, *Angelica archangelica*, are candied to provide the green cake and dessert decorations. This wild kind gives a yellow dye; it has stout, hollow stems, purple-tinted, 90–120 centimetres tall; often feathery leaves with toothed leaflets, and branching clusters of tiny white flowers (sometimes pink) appearing in July and August. The root, if chewed, was said to protect against witches. **Perennial**

Wild Carrot
(Daucus carota)

Fields/wasteland/hedgerows
Umbelliferae

Do not expect the root of this to be like the carrot you eat; it is whitish, hard and rather small, and tastes unpleasant and bitter. The vegetable was developed from this in the 16th century. Stems are about 60 centimetres tall, leaves very feathery, and flowers small and white, in many-flowered clusters, the centre flower in each being red or purple. Flowering time is from June to August. **Biennial**

Wild Chamomile
(Chamomilla recutita)

Fields/wasteland/hedgerows
Compositae

Daisy-like white flower petals surround a hollow yellow, conical centre. It flowers all summer, grows about 30 centimetres tall, often less, beside cornfields, and has very pinnate leaves. It smells aromatic when rubbed. **Annual**

SIX OR MORE PETALS

Waterlily
(Nymphaea alba)

Damp places/water
Nymphaceae

The large, white, many-petalled, cupped flowers which float on the water of lakes and ponds from June to September are Waterlilies. Their leaves are floating also, round but with a deep indentation where the stalk joins the leaf blade. The leaves are strong enough to bear a frog. **Perennial**

Wood Anemone
(Ranunculus nemorosa)

Shady places/woodland
Ranunculaceae

The word anemone comes from the Greek word *anemos*, which means wind; it was thought that the flowers opened with the first spring breeze, and they flower from March to May. Wood Anemones have 6–12 pointed white petals, looking like bells before they unfold, on delicate stems about 10 centimetres tall. The stalked leaves are in groups of three, each palmately lobed into five parts and with toothed edges. **Perennial**

FIVE PETALS

Black Nightshade
(Solanum nigrum)

Fields/wasteland/hedgerows
Solanaceae

About 30 centimetres tall, this is a bushy plant, but with soft, not woody, stems, and alternate, pointed ovate leaves. Small white flowers with pointed yellow centres (the stamens) come in small clusters from July to October, followed by round berries, first green, then black. All of the plant is poisonous, especially the berries. **Annual**

Chickweed
F 8-10mm x
▽

△
Burnet Rose
F 20-40mm x

Bladder Campion
△
F 12mm x

English Stonecrop
F 10mm x
◁

Grass of
Parnassus
F 20mm x
◁

Stitchwort
F 20-30mm x
▷

Sea Campion
F 20mm x
◁

Sundew
F 5mm x
◁

Strawberry ▽
F 15mm x

Bladder Campion
(Silene vulgaris)

Fields/wasteland/hedgerows
Caryophyllaceae

The stems are 15–30 centimetres tall, with long-ovate leaves in pairs, and clusters of a few flowers at the end of the stems. Each white flower has five, deeply two-lobed petals; blooming is from May to September. The 'bladder' at the back of the flower is the swollen calyx. The petals are often small and withered looking. **Perennial**

Burnet Rose
(Rosa pimpinellifolia)

Fields/wasteland/hedgerows
Rosaceae

Also called *Rosa spinosissima*, meaning extremely prickly, this is a shortish rose, up to 50 centimetres tall, with creeping stems rooting at the leaf joints, and white (sometimes pink), five-petalled flowers in June and July. It is very bristly; leaves have three to five pairs of toothed leaflets, and the hips are dark purple to black when ripe. **Perennial**

Chickweed
(Stellaria media)

Fields/wasteland/hedgerows
Caryophyllaceae

A fragile little plant, with delicate, easily broken stems 15–30 centimetres tall, small ovate leaves in pairs, and small white, star-like flowers on long stalks, with five deeply divided petals, appearing in spring, summer and autumn. It is a common vegetable garden weed; it gets its common name because its seeds are eaten a lot by birds. It was used to make ointments for rashes and inflammation. **Annual**

English Stonecrop
(Sedum anglicum)

Fields/wasteland/hedgerows
Crassulaceae

There are lots of Stonecrops which grow wild in stony places in northern Europe; this one has white, five-petalled, star-like flowers, about one centimetre wide, a few in a cluster at the top of the short, sometimes sprawling, 7 centimetre stems. It flowers from June to September. The fleshy, tiny leaves are almost round, tinted red, and crowded along the stems. **Perennial**

Grass of Parnassus

(Parnassia palustris)

Damp places/water
Parnassiaceae

Flowers appear from August to September and are 2 centimetres wide, with five strongly veined petals, one flower at the top of each 15–30 centimetre stem. The heart-shaped, stalked leaves form a rosette at the plant's base. **Perennial**

Sea Campion

(Silene vulgaris maritima)

Coast/seashore
Caryophyllaceae

This is very like the Bladder Campion but has a much prettier and larger flower. The five petals look frilled; they are more evenly arranged in a complete circle and the edges are scalloped rather than lobed. The leaves are small and thick, the stems shorter. It flowers in July and August. **Perennial**

Stitchwort

(Stellaria holostea)

Fields/wasteland/hedgerows
Caryophyllaceae

The stem is thin and straggling, about 60 centimetres tall, with narrow pointed leaves in pairs, and white, five-petalled flowers, each petal deeply notched, appearing from April to June. Seed pods are small, shiny and round. **Perennial**

Strawberry

(Fragaria vesca)

Fields/wasteland/hedgerows
Rosaceae

This looks like a small version of the cultivated plant. The stalked, toothed leaves are in three parts, and the white flowers have five petals, and are 1.5 centimetres wide, appearing in May and June, followed by red berries. **Perennial**

Sundew

(Drosera rotundifolia)

Damp places/water
Droseraceae

A carnivorous plant. The long-stalked leaves are round, with red hairs on the top side, coming directly from the soil. From June to August, five-petalled white flowers in a short spike appear at the top of 15 centimetre stems. The outer, sticky leaf hairs fold over insects caught on the inner ones. **Perennial**

Wood Sorrel
F 20-30mm x

Garlic Mustard
F 6mm x
▷

Hairy Bittercress
F up to 5mm x
▷

Goosegrass
F 3-4mm x

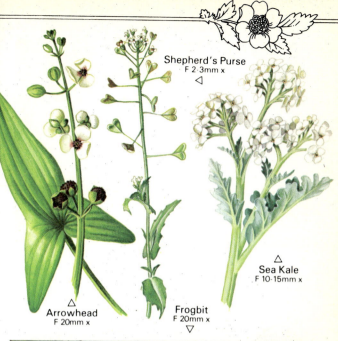

Shepherd's Purse
F 2-3mm x

Sea Kale
F 10-15mm x

Arrowhead
F 20mm x

Frogbit
F 20mm x

Wood Sorrel
(Oxalis acetosella)

Shady places/woodland
Oxalidaceae

Do not muddle this with the Wood Anemone; it has only five white, rounded petals, and leaves with three rounded leaflets, looking rather like clover leaves; each leaflet folds downwards along the midrib at night. Height is about 5–7 centimetres; flowering time is spring. The leaves contain a substance also found in common Sorrel, and Dock. **Perennial**

FOUR PETALS

Garlic Mustard (Jack-by-the-hedge) Shady places/woodland
(Alliaria petiolata)

Cruciferae

This grows 30–90 centimetres tall, and has alternately placed leaves (smelling of garlic), heart- or kidney-shaped, toothed at the edges, and about 6 centimetres wide. Rounded clusters of tiny white flowers grow at the top of the stems from April to July, and are followed by 5 centimetre long, narrow ribbed seed pods. **Biennial**

Goosegrass (Cleavers)
(Galium aparine)

Fields/wasteland/hedgerows
Rubiaceae

The seeds of this plant are the little round green balls which stick to your clothes if you brush against them. The stems can grow up to 180 centimetres tall, up into hedges and over other plants. The whole plant is covered in minute prickles, turned downwards, or hooked. The leaves are long and narrow, in whorls, up the stem; tiny white flowers appear just above the leaves between June and August. **Annual**

Hairy Bittercress
(Cardamine hirsuta)

Fields/wasteland/hedgerows
Cruciferae

This plant grows rapidly. It is small, only 7 or 10 centimetres tall, and at the base of the flowering stem is a rosette of pinnate leaves divided into four to seven pairs of leaflets. Tiny white flowers grow in a long cluster from March to November followed by long narrow seed pods. **Annual**

Sea Kale
(Crambe maritima)

Coast/seashore
Cruciferae

A low-growing, rather bushy plant, about 60 centimetres tall, with broad, thick, grey-green leaves, coarsely toothed and lobed, and four-petalled white flowers in stalked clusters from June to August. The seed pods are round, like peas. Sea Kale grows directly out of the sand or shingle, and the leaves were once eaten as a vegetable. **Perennial**

Shepherd's Purse
(Capsella bursa-pastoris)

Coast/seashore
Cruciferae

This can be found in bloom almost all year; it takes only a few weeks between the first shoot forming and flowering. The stems are 5–15 centimetres tall, the leaves narrow and deeply toothed or lobed, in a rosette at the base of the stem, and the tiny white flowers grow in stalked clusters. The seed pod is triangular, like an old-fashioned pouch. **Annual/biennial**

THREE PETALS

Arrowhead
(Sagittaria sagittifolia)

Damp places/water
Alismaceae

You will find this growing in ponds and shallow streams; its arrowhead-shaped leaves are 15–20 centimetres long, with the lower, pointed lobes of each leaf nearly as long as the main one. All the leaves stand up above the water. The flower stem is about 25–30 centimetres long, with three-petalled white flowers, purple-centred, from July to August. **Perennial**

Frogbit
(Hydrocharis morsus-ranae)

Damp places/water
Hydrocharitaceae

A pretty water-plant, with shiny, dark green, kidney-shaped leaves, rather thick, about 5 centimetres wide, and growing in tufts. The three-petalled rounded white flowers have a yellow centre, and bloom from July to August. The whole plant is floating and has long runners; it grows in ponds and ditches. *Morsus-ranae* is the Latin for 'bite' and 'frog'. **Perennial**

Eyebright
F 4mm x

Dead-nettle
F 20-25mm l

Lady's Tresses
F 7mm l
◁

White Helleborine
F 15-20mm l

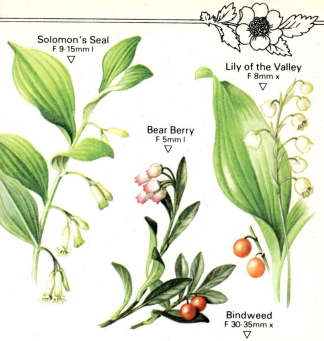

Solomon's Seal
F 9-15mm l
▽

Lily of the Valley
F 8mm x
▽

Bear Berry
F 5mm l
▽

Bindweed
F 30-35mm x
▽

TWO-LIPPED/PEAFLOWERS

Dead-nettle
(Lamium album)

Fields/wasteland/hedgerows
Labiatae

The leaves of Dead-nettle look very like those of the stinging Nettle, but are not painful to touch. It is much shorter, as well, growing 20–30 centimetres tall, with clusters of white, hooded flowers about one centimetre long, at intervals up the stem, just above the leaves, from March to June, and in autumn. It is slightly aromatic. **Perennial**

Eyebright
(Euphrasia rostkoviana)

Fields/wasteland/hedgerows
Scrophulariaceae

A small insignificant plant, easily missed, this is still used for curing minor eye troubles. The stem is 5–15 centimetres tall, with rounded leaves in pairs, much toothed, 6 millimetres wide, and white two-lipped flowers, marked with purple and a yellow patch, appearing from June to October. It is semi-parasitic, on grasses. **Annual**

Lady's Tresses
(Spiranthes spiralis)

Fields/wasteland/hedgerows
Orchidaceae

The flowers of this orchid do not appear until the leaves have withered. These are blue-green, oblong, about 3 centimetres long, and come at the base of the stem, which is 15–20 centimetres tall, beside the leaves. Scented white flowers grow to one side of a 5 centimetre long spike in August and September. Grows in dryish, grassy places. **Perennial**

White Helleborine
(Cephalanthera damsonium)

Shade/woodland
Orchidaceae

You are most likely to find this orchid in beechwoods, flowering in June and July. The alternate leaves are oblong, pointed and with the veins parallel to one another, and the creamy white flowers grow on upright stems in a loose spike. They are shaped like a globe, and hardly unfold. Height is about 30–45 centimetres. **Perennial**

BELL-SHAPED/OTHERS

Bear Berry
(Arctostaphylos uva-ursi)

High places/mountains
Ericaceae

Uva-ursi means the 'bear's-grape'; it has bright red edible berries. It is a tough, woody little plant with creeping stems forming a mat, and oblong, alternate, evergreen leaves 2 centimetres long. The white flowers have pink tips and are bell-shaped, a few in each cluster, appearing from April to June. **Perennial**

Bindweed
(Calystegia sepium)

Fields/wasteland/hedgerows
Convolvulaceae

Bindweed's white 5 centimetre long trumpets bloom in hedges and thickets from June to August. It is a climbing plant with twining stems, many metres long, and arrow-shaped, alternate leaves. The two green sepal-like bracts are pointed and enclose five sepals; do not confuse it with *Calystegia sylvatica*, which has two large, *rounded* bracts hiding the sepals. **Perennial**

Lily of the Valley
(Convallaria majalis)

Shady places/woodland
Liliaceae

The leaves of this plant look like those of Ramsons, broad-oval and pointed but, unlike it, the flowers have an extremely sweet fragrance. They grow in a one-sided spike in May, and are white and bell-like, with short stems, followed by red berries. Height is about 15 centimetres. The plant is poisonous.
Perennial

Solomon's Seal
(Polygonatum multiflorum)

Shady places/woodland
Liliaceae

The arching stems are 45–60 centimetres tall, with alternate, wavy-edged, long-oval leaves to one side, and hanging white bell flowers, one to three together, on the opposite side, in May and June. Its common name may be because the scars left on the rootstock where last year's stems died, were thought to look like the six-pointed star called this. **Perennial**

Red Flowers

Scarlet Pimpernel
F 8mm x
▽

Blood-red Geranium
F 25-30mm x
▷

Poppy
F 70-100mm x
▽

△
Great Burnet
Fh 20mm x

GROUPED FLOWERS

Great Burnet
(Sanguisorba officinale)

Fields/wasteland/hedgerows
Rosaceae

The 45–75 centimetre long stems have pinnate leaves with six pairs of deeply toothed leaflets, and tiny flowers in a ball about 2 centimetres wide, from June to September. Burnet comes from an old French word meaning 'brown cloth', in reference to the flower colour. **Perennial**

FIVE PETALS

Blood-red Geranium
(Geranium sanguineum)

Fields/wasteland/hedgerows
Geraniaceae

The deep red (sometimes red-purple) flowers with five rounded petals appear from July to August, singly, on long stalks. Leaves are palmately lobed, each of the five to seven lobes being cut into two or three small lobes at the ends. **Perennial**

Scarlet Pimpernel
(Anagallis arvensis)

Fields/wasteland/hedgerows
Gentianaceae

A mat-forming plant with creeping stems 15 centimetres and more long, and small pointed leaves in pairs. The red flowers are about 8 millimetres wide, with five rounded petals, opening in sunshine, and closing on cloudy days and at night. Flowering is between May and August. **Annual**

FOUR PETALS

Poppy
(Papaver rhoeas)

Fields/wasteland/hedgerows
Papaveraceae

The Poppy flowers in summer and autumn. It is roughly hairy, about 30 centimetres tall, with feathery leaves, deeply cut. The seed head forms a little cup with a scalloped lid on it, packed full of minute black seeds. **Annual**

Index

Page numbers in **bold** *refer to illustrations*

124